Joe L. P. Lugalla, Colleta G. Kibassa

Urban Life and Street Children's Health

Afrikanische Studien / African Studies

Volume 16

LIT

Joe L. P. Lugalla, Colleta G. Kibassa

Urban Life and Street Children's Health

Children's Accounts of Urban Hardships and Violence in Tanzania

LIT

Cover Picture: A street boy selling used shoes in Dar-es-Salaam

Bibliographic information published by Die Deutsche Bibliothek
Die Deutsche Bibliothek lists this publication in the Deutsche
Nationalbibliografie; detailed bibliographic data are available in the
Internet at http://dnb.ddb.de.

ISBN 3-8258-6690-4

© LIT VERLAG Münster – Hamburg – London   2003
Grevener Str./Fresnostr. 2   48159 Münster
Tel. 0251-23 50 91   Fax 0251-23 19 72
e-Mail: lit@lit-verlag.de   http://www.lit-verlag.de

Distributed in North America by:

Transaction Publishers
New Brunswick (U.S.A.) and London (U.K.)

Transaction Publishers   Tel.: (732) 445 - 2280
Rutgers University   Fax: (732) 445 - 3138
35 Berrue Circle   for orders (U. S. only):
Piscataway, NJ 08854   toll free (888) 999 - 6778

CONTENTS

List of Tables and Figures

Tables

Figures

iv

Abbreviations

AIDS:	Acquired Immunodeficiency Syndrome
CBOs:	Community Based Organizations
COBET:	Complementary Basic Education in Tanzania
DANIDA:	Danish International Development Agency
DUP:	Dar-es-Salaam University Press
GNP:	Gross National Product
HBS:	Household Budget Survey
IMF:	International Monetary Fund
MOEC:	Ministry of Education and Culture
NACP:	National AIDS Control Program
NGOs:	Non-Governmental Organizations
SAPs:	Structural Adjustment Programs
STDs:	Sexually Transmitted Diseases
SUVs:	Sports Utility Vehicles
TADREG:	Tanzania Development Research Group
TDHS:	Tanzania Demographic Health Studies
TAMWA:	Tanzania Women Media Association
TANU:	Tanzania African National Union
TAWLA:	Tanzania Association of Women Lawyers
TAZARA:	Tanzania Zambia Railway Authority
TCRS:	Tanzania Christian Rescue Centre
TGNP:	Tanzania Gender Networking Program
TSHS:	Tanzania Shillings
UNICEF:	United Nations Children's Education Fund
UPE:	Universal Primary Education
URT:	United Republic of Tanzania
USA:	United States of America
WTO:	World Trade Organization

Acknowledgements

A book like this is certainly not a product of the efforts of authors alone, but a result of concerted collaborative effort between individuals and institutions. The study that has generated this work was carried out in Tanzania by the authors between February 1999 and January 2001. We therefore wish to begin by acknowledging the generous financial support from the Harry Frank Guggenheim Foundation of New York, USA. It is this organization that funded our study from the beginning to the end. In particular, we would like to convey our sincere thanks to Karen Colvard, Senior Program Officer in the Foundation, for her constructive comments and support from the very beginning when our research project was being conceptualized and designed. We also convey our sincere gratitude and thanks to the Tanzania's Commission of Science and Technology for granting us permission to carry out a research project of this kind in Tanzania, and to the Dar-es-Salaam City Council for allowing us to carry out the study in their area of jurisdiction.

This study is unique in a variety of ways. First, it is an interdisciplinary research study involving researchers from diverse academic backgrounds. Joe Lugalla is a social scientist with an academic background in sociology, anthropology, and social medicine, while Colleta Kibassa is a consultant pediatrician with a focus on reproductive and child health. This interdisciplinary approach and collaboration was very helpful in understanding and addressing the interplay between urban life, social life of street children and their health. Secondly the study is a result of collaboration between two international institutions. Dr. Lugalla is a an associate professor at the University of New Hampshire in United States, and Dr. Kibassa is a consultant pediatrician in the Ministry of Health in Tanzania and also works as the Tanzania's National Coordinator of Integrated Management of Childhood Illnesses. We therefore wish to acknowledge the support of our institutions for supporting our collaborative work that has finally produced this book. The University of New Hampshire granted Joe Lugalla a one-semester leave of absence in the year 2000 so that he could fully participate in the fieldwork in Tanzania. At the same time, Dr. Kibassa had to devote a portion of her official time with the Ministry of Health so that she could focus on this project. There is no doubt that without this kind of support from our employers, this collaborative work would have been cumbersome and almost impossible. We therefore appreciate their help and say thank you. While in our fieldwork, we were assisted by twenty students (females and males) from the Department of Sociology at the University of Dar-es-Salaam. These students worked tirelessly as research assistants, collecting data and interviewing street children. The research assistants were the visible face of our project to the street children. We cannot list their names here, but we wish to acknowledge their support for without their tireless efforts we two alone could have not managed to interview more than four hundred street children and at the same collect other relevant information from other sources. If we have succeeded in documenting clearly to the readers what we intended to, it is indeed because of their presence and

vi

support.

In the course of carrying out this study and finally in the process of writing the book, we have benefited from the support of many people and institutions in Tanzania. First and foremost, we wish to acknowledge the support and encouragement we received from various officers of the following institutions: The Ministry of Education and Culture, the Ministry of Labour and Youth, The Ministry of Health, the Office of the Vice President, and, especially, the Directorate of Poverty Eradication. We also acknowledge a variety of ideas gleaned from discussions with different academic members of the Department of Sociology and Faculty of Law at the University of Dar-es-Salaam. In particular we would like to mention Dr. Felician Tungaraza, Dr. Abu Mvungi, Dr. Joachim Abunuwas Mwami, Dr. Christopher Comoro and Dr. Lutfried Mbunda. We also would like to convey our special thanks to Dr. Guerino Chalamila, the Doctor –in- Charge of the Dar-es-Salaam Youth Clinic for providing us with data that has assisted us significantly in understanding the health conditions of most youth, including street children, who live in Dar-es-Salaam. In United States of America, we have benefited from the input of Professors Steve Reyna, Nina Glick Schiller, Charles Bolian, Justus Ogembo and Funso Afolayan, all from the University of New Hampshire. The ideas of Professor Charles Green of Hunter College in New York and Professor Kris Heggenhougen of the School of Public Health at Boston University and Saidi Kapiga of the School of Public Health at Harvard have also been of great help to us in shaping our ideas while we were engaged in this project.

In order to exchange ideas and to enhance our research process, we also organized an International Conference on Street Children and Street Children's Health in Dar-es-Salaam in April 2000. The conference brought participants from USA, Italy, Australia, New Zealand, Kenya, Uganda, and South Africa. We benefited immensely from these participants and we would like to take this opportunity to say thank you to all of them. The conference was supported by the Center for Humanities at the University of New Hampshire, the Wenner Gren Foundation for Anthropological Research of New York, and Plan International (Tanzania Office). We would like to take this opportunity to thank them all for this support. Finally, Stephanie Smith, Carolyn Stolzenberg, Jennifer Beard. Marina Pesa , Amanda Willette and Lisa Feldman Massey all from the University of New Hampshire, have been helpful in one way or another in the final production of this work. We highly appreciate their support.

We especially extend our gratitude to the street children of Dar-es-Salaam themselves. They spent much of their valuable time talking to us. We have learned much from their narratives as well as from their joy and suffering. We have decided to honor them by producing this book so that other people can understand their situation and assume responsibility for finding ways in which these children can be assisted. We apologize to all street children if we have not succeeded in presenting this picture in the way they wanted. Although this work has profited from ideas and support of several individuals, the weaknesses that can be noted in this work are entirely ours. This book is about

Street Children of Tanzania. We therefore dedicate it to them with the hope that their suffering will end soon.

Chapter 1

The Background and the Setting of the Study

1.1 Introduction

"If I was a school girl, I could say don't bother me, I want my education. If I had a business, I could say I was a businesswoman. If I had lived in a home then they would not think of me (sexually) because they would know I had parents." (Narrative from a street girl in Mwanza, Tanzania, Kudrati and Rajani 1996)

"I decided to leave my home because my parents could not take care of me...We are seven. We survive by eating leftovers. Sometimes you don't feel like eating leftovers. They are spoilt and have pungent smell. You wait for the next day hoping to get something better...but crumbs is the stuff we (street boys) cannot do without. We have to do some odd jobs to get some money. Moreover, stealing is part of the game and frankly speaking, we do this because circumstances turn us wild." (Narrative from a street boy in Dar-es-Salaam, Tanzania, Lugalla 1995b)

"We as street children, have no life at all. Life is meaningless to us. We experience a variety of hardships and violent acts from adults, law enforcement institutions and from ordinary people. We are living only physically, but in fact we are dead already. We do not care. Come what may. We are forced to commit crimes. Getting arrested or killed by mob justice while stealing is just like an accident at work place. We have to survive. We steal because we need to eat." (Street boy response during fieldwork in Dar-es-Salaam City 2000)

The above are narratives from Tanzanian street children. These narratives portray in brief how street children survive and experience street life. Trying to understand these children and the hardships they experience in urban streets was the subject matter of this study. Since early 1980s, the sub-Saharan African countries have experienced social and economic crises characterized by internal and external debt, declining terms of trade, inflation, high cost of living and increasing poverty. This situation has severely threatened the welfare of children, and other vulnerable social groups. In order to respond to the social economic crisis, most countries have since mid 1980s been involved in economic reforms by implementing Structural Adjustment Programs (SAPs) which have been imposed by World Bank and International Monetary Fund (IMF) as a cure to the economic crisis. However, recent studies on the impact of these policies reveal that adjustment policies requiring governments to reduce spending, devalue their local currency, improve trade balances, meet debts, privatize state owned economic sectors and liberalize trade have led to significant decreases in funds for health, education and other social programs for vulnerable social groups (Cornea 1987, Lugalla 1997, Mlawa and Green 1998). Additional studies are beginning to show how epidemics often appear in conjunction with economic and political crises (Schoepf 1996, Lugalla *et al.* 1999, Kapiga and Lugalla 2001). Further, most of these studies have confirmed that these policies generate poverty rather than social and economic development. In sum, instead of fixing the problems, World Bank/IMF programs have exacerbated them. It is also increasingly evident that these macro-level economic and political crises produce micro-level social dislocations.

While most of these macro-level trends have been documented, the complex ways in which they affect vulnerable social groups on the micro-level like children and women has only begun to be understood. Thus, we already have quantitative information that shows how many children die due to organized political violence (wars) every year, how many die or become ill due to poverty related factors, how many are enrolled in school and how many finish, how many drop out and how many suffer from mild to severe malnutrition. We also have rough information that shows how many children have abandoned their poor violent families or have been abandoned and are now living on their own in urban streets.

These problems have been recognized and researched earlier in countries like Columbia and Brazil in South America and India and Philippines in Asia (Knaul 1995, Rizzini 1994, Patel 1990, Porio 1990), though they have hardly been eradicated. Similar problems are now recognized to be rampant in sub-Saharan Africa. However, systematic studies are lacking for Africa to explain how existing world conditions, together with African processes of social transformation, are creating a relatively unhealthy, and troubled population of young people who are growing up with more severe problems than ever before.

This social deterioration is chronic in cities in sub-Saharan Africa. For example, since 1980s, besides problems of unemployment, housing and other social services, sub-Saharan African cities have been confronted with another social problem of the rapid increasing rate of unsupervised young children living in the streets on their own. The increasing number of children dying from poverty, and organized and unorganized street violence is alarming; yet, due to lack of detailed information about this social problem, most governments have ended up formulating policies that harm these children more than help them. The numbers of children living in urban streets continue to increase and to experience the grimmest hardships and violence. It is, as the narrative at the beginning of this section suggests, a world of struggle for "crumbs...we cannot do without." Because the number of street children is increasing and efforts of non-governmental organizations are also on the increase, street children are now commanding a great deal of attention in Africa.

It is this situation that motivated us to design this study. The aim of this study was to deepen our understanding of the street children and their street life in sub-Saharan Africa. We began by trying to understand the factors that create street children and proceeded to an in-depth understanding of the nature of street life itself in order to understand how street children survived, the kind of hardships and violence they experienced, how this life affected their health and social life, and how they developed coping mechanisms on the one hand and social behavior on the other.

1.2 Statement of the Problem

During the past ten years, Tanzanian cities have undergone rapid changes that have transformed the urban environment and the lives of millions of urban dwellers [1]. These changes affect almost everyone, but particularly the urban poor. Some of the growing social problems associated with these changes include escalating rates of unemployment, increasing crime rates, organized and unorganized violence, and a tremendous increase (especially in the last decade) of unsupervised children either living alone or working on urban streets. This problem is especially acute in big cities like Dar-es-Salaam, Arusha, Dodoma, Morogoro, Moshi, Tanga, Mbeya, and Mwanza where urban population growth has exploded amidst intensifying and severe social and economic crises. The majority of these children have, for various reasons, either abandoned or have been abandoned by their families and have migrated to urban areas in order to earn a living. Their rapid increase in number, their modes of survival and the problems they experience at a time when Tanzania is experiencing great financial constraints raise concerns and calls for immediate attention.

Most politicians and policy planners see urban street children in a negative light, considering them as hooligans, vagabonds and criminals. There are many cases of street children being repatriated to their rural homes, detained, and sometimes beaten by police. Most official policies have been correctional, repressive, and aimed more at social control than social development. They have viewed poor children on streets as a threat to safety and rehabilitation in institutions as the best solution. As a result, these policies have dealt only with the symptoms of the problem rather than their real causes.

Why is this so? One reason for the failure of the government to provide viable solutions to this problem stems from the fact that the government is ignorant about the nature of street children and street life in Tanzania. There have been *no* attempts to establish any in-depth and systematic studies aimed at understanding these children in terms of: (i) who they are, (ii) where they come from, (iii) their reasons for leaving their home, (iv) how they survive and meet their daily needs, (v) what kind of hardships and types of violence they experience and, (vi) how they surmount these problems.

1.3 The Aims and Objectives of the Study

In view of the above problem, the aims and objectives of this study were to address these problems of ignorance by conducting an in-depth rigorous investigation of street children and their street life in order to acquire a knowledge base that can be used to formulate policy and programs to address the problems of street children. We were particularly interested in documenting the kind of hardship and violence that these children experienced, how these affected them, and how they coped with the situation.

In order to situate our analysis within the context of political economy, we decided to focus on a variety of objectives. Our first objective was to identify social, economic and political processes that generate and perpetuate the increasing number of street children. Our second objective was to understand the nature of these children particularly in terms of their socio-economic background. Third, we explored their basic daily needs and how they meet them. Fourth, we were interested in the kind of problems street children confront and how they surmount them? Our fifth objective was to assess how street life in general impacts children's behavior and health. Finally, we wanted to gage how street children's survival or coping mechanisms vary by gender.

1.4 Significance and Justification

The rationale and justification of our study stems from the fact that studies on street children in sub-Saharan Africa are rare, ad hoc or are just emerging. Existing studies have been weak in the following ways: First, they have made no distinction between children who work on streets during the day and return to their families in the evening and those who physically work and live on streets, between those who are part of the informal work force and those ones who engage in illegal activities. These studies do not distinguish between children who maintain family ties and those who

4

have lost all contact with their families, and between those who plan their own income generating activities and those who work on the street in family related enterprises. Furthermore, existing research has tended to look at children in a vacuum and not as part of the social system. Because of these shortcomings, blanket policy recommendations have treated street children as a single, homogenous category. As a result, policies have often ended up hurting most street children rather than helping them.

Secondly, very little is known about the kind of economic activities the children are engaged in and how they are organized. It is also unclear how some children are linked to organized crime. In most countries of sub-Saharan Africa the media have been heavy-handed in their coverage of criminality among street children, fueling prejudice and reinforcing the commonly held view that they are a serious danger to society. What is considered as "rehabilitation" of juvenile offenders has not advanced much beyond imprisonment. In some countries these rehabilitation centers have been characterized by brutality, abuse and violence against the very children they are supposed to rehabilitate. We as researchers strongly insist that research is needed in sub-Saharan African countries to deflate the myth that every child on the street is a criminal and therefore a threat to society. We need detailed studies on this subject to determine the root causes of the problem, to understand the nature of street life and to suggest remedying solutions that have policy implications.

Third, data concerning the influence of gender on children and street life are virtually nonexistent. Studies have paid little attention to factors pushing girls into streets, how they live, how they relate to one another, the problems they experience and how they surmount them. For example, do girls leave home for the same reasons as boys? Are girls leaving their homes because of new roles their families are imposing on them, such as arranged marriages and greater workloads than their male counterparts? How are unequal gender relations, characterized by dominant patriarchal social relations, shaping these processes? We believe studies that examine these issues will lead to formulation of policies that are not gender blind.

Fourth, physical violence, street gang violence, sexual abuse, domestic and drug related violence, psychological hardships, and stresses these children experience have been only superficially addressed in previous studies. No attempts have been made to see how these factors affect children's social life and health and how experiences of hardships and violence vary by gender. Studies in Brazil have found that because of the conditions of violence and insecurity children face, they tend to look out mainly for themselves. Is the same trend happening in sub-Saharan Africa? If so, how can one use children's own initiatives in dealing with security or earning a living to help formulate policies which can benefit these children?

5

Fifth, most street children studies in Africa have tended to study children in a vacuum and not within the context of political economy. The relationship between social and economic crises and structural adjustments and their impacts upon families and children is only now coming to be understood. Families of the urban and rural poor are undergoing significant transformation and nuclear families, particularly single female-headed ones, are becoming increasingly frequent. There is concrete evidence showing how SAPs are destroying families and communities. There is also growing evidence that economic crisis is leading to a situation where social networks of assistance within the extended family are diminishing significantly in the urban context. What is not clear is how this happens, and whether it is contributing to generating street children, and if so how.

Sixth, most studies have only been implemented by social scientists. They have not been interdisciplinary. Because of this, they have not been able to assess the impact of street life. This study was interdisciplinary and was carried out by a social scientist and a health specialist. By dealing with the above issues, we believe that this study has ultimately attempted to address the weaknesses of previous studies and therefore provides comprehensive information that will expand our understanding of the nature of street children and street life in Tanzania. We have no doubts that this information is essential for policies that can help to provide a long-term solution to this problem.

1.5 Research Methodology
i) Theoretical Framework

Since the early 1980s, as part of an increasing concern on the impact of social economic crisis on communities and families in sub-Saharan Africa, many studies have sought to document how macro-level crises influence micro-level dislocations. These confirm that policies at national level impact families and communities at local levels. A recent study by Weisner on the changing nature of African families and communities has argued that these changes often involve losing resources and forms of power to delocalized forces that are part of a wider world system (Weisner 1997). In view of such findings, studies that analyze changes in the distribution of political and economic power have gained ground during the past recent years. Many writers have been using this kind of approach in analyzing social, economic and political problems confronting sub-Saharan Africa (Lesthaeghe 1989, Mutuku and Mutiso 1994, Lugalla 1995ab, Schoepf 1996, Weisner 1997).

This theoretical framework is equally relevant to our understanding of the problem of street children in this part of Africa. We used it in order to see how policies implemented at national level impact communities and families, and how they create conditions that generate street children. There are sometimes universal problems

6

facing all families and communities in raising children. Le Vine *et al.* 1994), argue that four adaptive needs (subsistence, reproduction, communication, and social regulation) shape human childcare and that these are always socially and culturally organized. The most important challenge facing families and communities everywhere is to provide a daily routine of life for children that is relatively stable and sustainable. How are families and communities in Tanzania facing this challenge? Since in most sub-Saharan African countries the problem of street children became apparent in early 1980s (the beginning years of the economic crisis) and became serious in mid 1980s to date (the period of structural adjustments and economic reforms), among the factors that have been considered influential in generating this problem are the economic crisis and the impact of SAPs. It is believed that the economic crisis and SAPs have destroyed communities and families socially and economically, and by doing so, they have created conditions necessary for the development of this problem.

The basic tenets of SAPs in sub-Saharan Africa have been: (a) devaluation of local currencies, (b) trade liberalization, (c) lifting of price controls and institution of incentives, (d) removal of subsidies, (e) reduction of government expenditure in social services and introduction of user charges in these services, and (f) privatization of government-owned economic sector institutions. These policies have affected negatively the poor and vulnerable groups by shifting government resources away from social services and poverty alleviation (Manundu 1992a). The cost of living is high and user charges in social services have increased the burden of the already overburdened poor. Many youth growing up without education, skills, or job prospects face bleak futures and can only live for the moment. As a result, most of them migrate to cities in search of a better life. In families hard pressed to sell more produce, women's labor is most easily harnessed in rural Africa, for they are seldom able to refuse patriarchal authority. In some cases, this forces young girls to seek escape from rural drudgery by migrating to the city. In some families, whose economic well-being has been destroyed by the crisis and SAPs, the traditional African family social networks of assistance become severe or disappear, forcing children to leave their families. For example, men whose incomes are low and uncertain, or who become unemployed and hopeless, are frequently unwilling to assume responsibility for children. In families suffering from material want and psychological stress, alcoholism and violence increase, while marriage ties, already tenuous for many, become more fragile (Schoepf 1997). This increases the double burden of women as producers and reproducers since in such situations women have to take care of children as single parents (Lugalla 1995a). It is also increasingly evident that the traditional African land tenure system that was until recently still somehow egalitarian is moving toward unequal land tenure systems due to SAPs. Many people in rural and urban areas are

7

currently losing their land due to policies that advocate privatization (URT 1992). Since land is a source of livelihood to most people in Tanzania, becoming landless has put some families into destitution, a situation that is conducive to creating street children. Given the above observations, our study was structured around the following two main hypotheses:

(a) That family resource decline leads to a situation whereby street children are generated. The hypothesis proposed that family resource decline was inversely related to the number of street children. Specifically, the conjuncture of economic crisis and structural adjustment policies produce declines in income, durable asset, and other resources to families, their kin support networks, and their local community support networks. These resource declines lead to family resource levels at/or below culturally and nutritionally defined subsistence levels. Increases in numbers of families with subsistence or sub-subsistence resource levels provoke greater numbers of children in these families to take to the streets.

Figure 1: Hypothesis A: Family Resource and Street Children

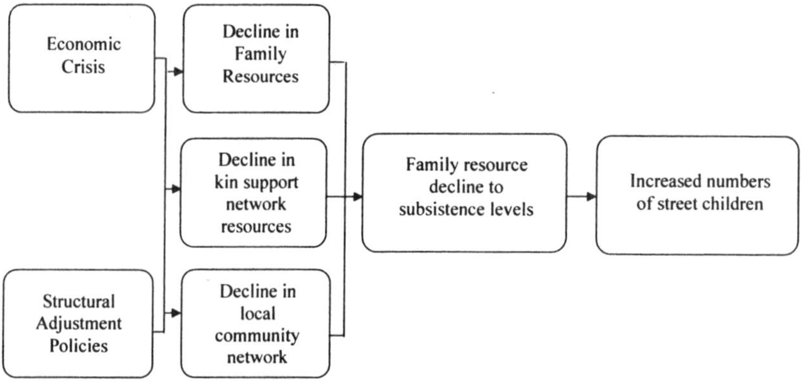

(b) Resource attainment leads to identity among street children. This hypothesis proposes that the more a street child is able to attain resources in a culturally appropriate manner the more her or his individual identity will be maintained. Specifically, street children scan their environment for culturally appropriate resource opportunities, which lead them to attempt these opportunities. If the street child experiences the attainment of resources in a culturally appropriate manner, then her or

8

his identity is likely to be reinforced. If the street child only occasionally experiences the attainment of resources in a culturally appropriate manner, then her or his identity is likely to be at risk, with there being increased probability of physical and psychological disorder. If the street child experiences little resource attainment and/or either symbolic or physical violence, then her or his identity is likely to undergo deculturation, so that, literally not knowing who or what she or he is, severe psychological disorder is probable.

Figure 2: Hypothesis B: Resource Attainment and Identity Among Street Children

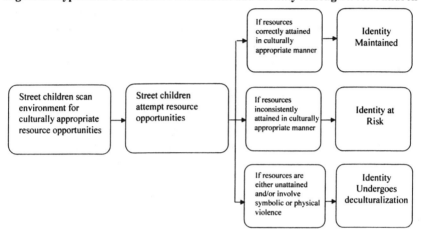

ii) Area of the Study

Our study was based in Dar-es-Salaam City, Tanzania. We chose this city for the following reasons. Dar-es-Salaam, with an approximate population of 4-5 million, is the largest city in Tanzania. Since colonization, this city has lead in terms of urban population growth and has accommodated more than one third of all urban dwellers in the country for over the last three decades (Lugalla 1995b). Dar-es-Salaam is the biggest industrial city in Tanzania. It is also the most famous commercial center and is also the center of Tanzania's politics.

Dar-es-Salaam is divided into three administrative municipal districts namely: Temeke, Ilala and Kinondoni. Recent information from UNICEF (Dar-es-Salaam office) shows that there are approximately 5000 street children in Tanzania of whom 40% live in Dar-es-Salaam.

9

iii) Research Design and Method of Data Collection

Our field research lasted for two years (1999-2000). We divided the two years into different project phases involving different research components. In year one (1999), our research plan was divided into two main phases. Similar to other traditional research projects, the first phase (February-May 1999) was for an in-depth literature review of information about street children in Tanzania. The second phase of year one (June-November 1999) involved the following two main activities. First, we began by visiting different government offices that issue policies and coordinate social-work-related activities with street children. We also met development planners, social workers, probation officers and the police so that we could learn from their experience. We also visited a variety of street children non-governmental organizations (NGOs) and their rehabilitation centers where we talked with street children who have been resettled in these centers. This phase assisted us in identifying different types of street children.

First, we decided to use the UNICEF categorization of street children namely, the "children **of** the street" and the "children **on** the street" in order to identify street children for our in-depth studies and locate their urban areas of operation. Second, after identifying these children, we sampled a total of 403 children and followed them up in their areas of operation for a period of almost one year. We began collecting data in the field in Temeke District in August 1999.

Year two (2000) of our research project was divided into three main phases. The first phase of four months (February-May) involved the collection of data in Ilala District, and the second four-month phase (June-September) was devoted to data collection in Kinondoni. The remaining three months (October-December 2000) were spent analyzing and reporting data).

Throughout our study, our methodology was mainly qualitative. We also used some quantitative methods in order to supplement and confirm some qualitative statements. A survey questionnaire was also used in order to collect some demographic information of street children and their socio-economic characteristics. We used a variety of ethnographic research methods including in-depth interviews with research subjects, participant and non-participant observation, recording life histories of street children and their stories about street life experience, and focus groups discussions. This intensive ethnographic study was aimed at understanding more completely the factors that put children into streets and their experience of street life. These methods allowed us to be close with street children, a situation that enabled us to feel, experience and sense the nature of street life.

Our entire research process treated children as active participants in the whole exercise. We made sure that we followed what the late Jonathan Mann echoed in 1992 at the International Conference on Street Youth in Rio de Janeiro:

"How we think of children and youth will determine our ability to communicate with them, for it will determine whether we talk to them, or with them; whether we are lecturing or whether we are engaged in dialogue. Communication with children and youth has its special features and characteristics; the essential challenge for us is to find ways of expanding the dialogue, and the direction of greater inclusiveness and more meaningful—rather than token—participation." (Jonathan Mann, Second International Conference on Street Youth, Rio de Janeiro, 1992)

In supporting Mann's position, we used a participatory dimension in our research in which street children participated as subjects of research rather than objects. We organized them into different focus groups discussions in order to enable them to share ideas about their historical background and their street life experiences. By spending most of our time with children and giving them more opportunity to talk, we were able to see the everyday experience of street children in distress through children's own eyes and from their own point of view. Focus group discussions also enabled us to establish links between communities and children and to ascertain certain general ideas about people's attitudes toward street children and street life. This enabled children to have their own voice. Since making street children talk to a stranger is not an easy exercise, we always began our field work in a new area by introducing our research in meetings with both community members and street children themselves in order to discuss the purpose of our project and to see how children themselves were going to participate in discussing several aspects of street children and street life. At the start of our work, our unique protocol of exchange with

11

street children was guided by the basic principle that researchers are there to learn from street children and not to teach or direct. We always created an atmosphere where children would generate questions and give stories about issues related to their background and experiences of street life.

We recruited male and female research assistants from the University of Dar-es-Salaam in order to facilitate easy response to questions that were gender sensitive. In order to establish a good relationship with street children, we trained our research assistants to be our study project's visible face. We prepared them for community involvement, and made sure that they were well-grounded in community participation techniques. They were supposed to acknowledge the fact that their fieldwork consisted of gaining trust from street children, and that they were expected to smooth over problem areas, notably dealing with fearful children and reluctant or would-be hostile informants. During the research process, the research assistants observed, participated in some street children activities, socialized with them, interviewed them and solicited more information without imposing anything that participants might feel uneasy.

Through these methods we gained a better understanding of how street children cope with street life by gender. We monitored the kind of activities children are engaged in and the hardships and violence they experience. We also assessed the nature of communication between children, how they create social relationships and how they plan their daily activities. Besides talking with children, we also talked with some urban families in order to understand how they perceived the economic problems caused by structural adjustments. We also assessed the kind of social networks at community level in order to see the potential of community-based initiatives in dealing with the problem of street children.

The ethnographic analysis served the following purposes: First, it assisted us in understanding processes of social change, experience and adaptation focusing on how Tanzania's social processes of change have lead to a situation where children are being thrown onto streets. Second, it also assisted us to study how street life-affects children's health, social life and social behavior, and how these children cope with the situation.

Our final analysis of these findings proceeded on two levels. We coded the ethnographic data separately. The quantitative material was entered in the computer and analyzed by using Microsoft Excel and SPSS statistical packages. Finally, we assessed the nature of association of different variables identified in quantitative data with ethnographic material. Considerable emphasis was given to qualitative analysis in order to provide "real life" explanations and illustrations of the linkages and processes observed and to interpret quantitative findings (Miles and Huberman 1984, Branner 1992).

1.6 How the Book is Organized

The book begins with the first chapter in which we discuss the background of the study as well as some methodological issues mentioning how the study was conceptualized, designed and operationalized. The second chapter is more or less a review of literature. What we do here is to situate the problem of street children as a global problem. We examine the nature of the problem in different countries, albeit in brief, and discuss how other countries are addressing the problem. In order to situate the problem of street children in a social historical context, we have devoted chapter three for an in-depth analysis of processes of social change, urbanization and the development of conditions of poverty in Tanzania. The eventual findings of this study are discussed in chapters four, five and six. While in chapter four we look specifically at the nature of street children in Tanzania, their stories and narratives about urban hardships and violence are discussed in chapter five. In chapter six we examine how street life affects street children's health.

In an attempt to explain how processes of social change are impacting Tanzanian families and their ability to take care of their children we decided to discuss education and the processes of socialization of children in chapter seven. In chapter eight we examine how the Tanzanian government has reacted to this problem. We examine the strengths and weaknesses of the official policies that focus at addressing this problem. Since this is a problem that is confronting the entire society, examining only what the government is doing is not enough. Therefore, we have decided to analyze in chapter nine how the civil society is reacting to the problem. What we have done here is to identify the kind of programs and strategies that have been established by the civil society in order to deal with the problem of street children. We also discuss the strengths as well as the weaknesses of these programs. Our book ends in chapter ten where we provide both long-term and short-term solutions to the problem.

Chapter 2

Street Children as a Global Problem

2.1 Introduction

"'Do you know that this is bad for your health?' I heard the juvenile officer say to Drigo with concern. 'Do you know that crack drives your hunger and fear away?'" Drigo shot back at the officer, 'And it's soooo fun!' he said chuckling. 'This stuff will kill you soon,' the officer retorted, shaking his head. 'Unless a bullet does it first,' Drigo said casually, looking at his own reflection on a windowpane and fixing his black wavy hair." (Marcelo Diversi *et al.* 1999).

While sharing her first impression in her well-known film *Salaam Bombay*, Mira Nair wrote the following note: "The taxi stopped at a red light on the Bandra flyover," and

"Within moments, I was surrounded by street children of all ages performing, begging, blowing soap bubbles, dancing, washing windows with a dirty rag–anything for a few praise. In the center of the intersection, I could see a fifteen year-old boy, his torso rising from maimed legs that rested on a wooden platform on wheels pushing himself by his hands from car to car, his skinny fingers stretching into each car window, begging. The light changed to green. I was terrified of what might happen to him now, surrounded as he was by trucks, cars, scooters, rickshaws. The boy caught hold of the back of the scooter, carried himself along at top speed until he reached the edge of the road, and there, propelled by sheer momentum, pirouetted flamboyantly, his hands raised skywards, saluting the deafening applause of an imaginary audience." (ibid.)

The problem of street children is not at all new. The factors that drive them into the streets, their coping mechanisms and the attitude of government officials as well as members of the public have attracted consideration. The problem is not peculiar to developing countries, but is also common in developed industrialized countries and in former socialist/communist countries currently making a transition toward capitalism. The "rent-boys" of London's railway terminals and the homeless children in many major cities in the United States are a case in point. The presence of street children in many countries of the world is one of the adverse consequences of urbanization, urban and rural poverty, and the failure of many governments in addressing the needs of marginalized social groups and other atrocities associated with social relations of inequality.

The number of street youth and children worldwide is hotly debated, with estimates ranging from several million to over 100 million (UNICEF 1989 and 1993, Raffaeli and Larson 1999). The imprecise numbers offered in regard to the street children population are due to the lack of thorough, in-depth research studies and to definitional problems of who is a street child.

For example, on one hand, there are the children "of" the street, most of whom have neither homes nor contact with their families or relatives. On the other hand, there are the children "on" the street, most of whom work long hours in the streets during the day and return to their homes at night. Contrary to the first group, these children have homes and enjoy the parental love and security of their relatives. Recently, and more so in cities in sub-Saharan Africa, we are witnessing a growing number of children accompanied by their parents (beggars) who survive by begging. In most cases, both the parents and the children are homeless.

According to Jacqueline Smollar (1999), in the United States homeless youth are defined as individuals less than nineteen years of age who meet at least one of the following criteria (Smollar, 1999).

• They have run away from their homes or from their alternative care placements and remained away for a long period of time with little or no connection with their families or caretakers.

• They have been pushed out of their homes or foster care placements, have been abandoned by their parents, or have left home for the streets with their parents' knowledge and consent.

• They have no stable place of residence; lack adult supervision, guidance, and care; and have little likelihood of reunification with parents.

Smollar argues that although the number of homeless youth in United States is not known, estimates range from 100,000 to 500,000 (Dietz and Coburn 1991, Smollar 1999). These homeless youth live in environments that often differ considerably from those of their peers who reside with families or in alternative care placements. The kind of environments in which these adolescents spend their teenage years may have a significant impact on their developmental outcomes (Smollar 1999).

2.2 Street Children in the Developing World

The fact that the problem of street children has been documented in both developed and developing countries does not necessarily mean that the magnitude of the problem is the same. There is increasing evidence that the situation is more appalling in developing countries. In these countries, due to increasing social and economic crisis, more children will be born into poverty, will be born prematurely, will die in the first year of life, will suffer from low birth weight, and will have mothers receiving late or no prenatal care. In the city of Sao Paulo, Brazil, there are about 500,000 street children, and it is estimated that approximately four fifths of Sao Paulo's prison inmates are former street children (Shorter and Onyancha 1999). In Calcutta, India, there are close to 300,000 street children. And in Africa, particularly sub-Saharan Africa, where approximately 70% of the population live below poverty levels, the specter of the street children is a growing one (ibid). Street children in Africa are a recent development, but their situation frequently reflects patterns of exploitation emanating from colonialism in the early Twentieth Century (Kilbride *et al.* 2001). In South Africa, all street children are of African origin, with no white children on the streets, a fact reflective of South Africa's history of racial segregation and apartheid (Kilbride *et al.* 2001, Le Roux 1996). Kenya, too, has neither Asian nor European street children, a reflection of racism during colonialism up to the early 1960s (Kilbride *et al.* 2001). In Africa, there is a close association between increasing family poverty and the magnitude of the problem of street children. There are specific macro causes that are associated with the dramatic rise in Africa's street children along with the poverty of global economic and structural adjustment forces (Kilbride *et al.* 2001). Some of these factors include civil war and famine, such as in Ethiopia, Sudan, Burundi and the Democratic Republic of Congo. At the same time, HIV/AIDS is also responsible for creating a large number of street children that are seen in African cities.

A study in Nairobi, Kenya has recently observed that street children in Nairobi tend to come from poor, female-headed households in slum or squatter areas (Mutuku and Mutiso 1994). A study of 400 street children in Nairobi in 1994 found that 90% were 6-15 years of age and that about 10% were over 15 (Suda 1994, Shorter and Onyancha 1999). About 50% of these children were born in the slums of Nairobi and the other half came from rural areas (ibid). Another study of 634 street children and 32 parents in Nairobi, Mombasa, Kisumu, Narok and Kitui urban centers of Kenya in 1990 noted similar observations (Shorter and Onyancha 1999). These studies noted that most street children came from single-parent families, which means, in most cases, from single mothers. They have little or no formal education, and therefore little prospect of a stable source of income (ibid). A study by Philista Onyango noted that parents of street children were unemployed; only 15% of the fathers had permanent employment, 44% were in irregular employment, temporary employment and self-employment, or else were subsistence farmers with fluctuating incomes (Onyango 1990, Shorter and Onyancha 1999). These findings concur with Blanc's argument

16

that street children are more likely to have an unemployed or severely underemployed parent, have had a parent jailed, endure substandard housing, suffer child abuse, drop out of primary school, and never attend secondary school or a university (Blanc Szanton 1994). They are more likely to be forced to work in an exploitative setting, get involved in substance abuse, enter prostitution, be exposed to repeated violence, and be affected by armed conflict (ibid). In addition, especially in Africa, many children are increasingly becoming orphans due to HIV/AIDS. These problems have been well documented in the countries of South America, especially in Brazil and Colombia (Rizzini 1994, Knaul 1995), but very few studies concentrate on Africa (Ishumi 1984, Mutuku and Mutiso 1994, Lugalla 1995b, Kudrati and Rajani 1996, Lugalla and Mbwambo 1998). Existing studies on street children have concentrated on the acquisition of elementary survey data, such as street children's age, gender, place of origin, social and economic characteristics, basic factors that push or pull them into the streets, and how they survive. There is no doubt that information derived from these questions forms a useful first step in designing research and policy. For example, it has allowed UNICEF and other agencies to categorize street children on the basis of the frequency with which they operate, live or sleep on the street and the degree of contact they maintain with their families.

In Brazil, where several studies of street children have been conducted, Rizzini, in "Brazil: A New Concept of Childhood," noted there was a general consensus that the majority of children who lead a street life come from poor families who often count on their children's earnings for survival. A similar observation has been noted in Columbia and India (Knaul 1995, Patel 1990). Mutuku and Mutiso (1994) and Lugalla (1995b) have also observed the same phenomena in Kenya and Tanzania respectively. In Brazil, Rizzini also argues that, contrary to popular belief, the majority of urban poor children on the streets of Brazilian cities live in two-parent families, although both are not necessarily their own parents. Her findings further reveal that most children "on" or "of" the street come from nuclear families; however, a significant number of their families are female-headed, and only a small percentage of these children have severed all contact or maintained only intermittent contact with their families. She has observed that the authorities often consider the families of poor children to be irresponsible, but has also countered that this indictment ignores the social causes that have marginalized a significant part of the urban population and have forced them into a full-time struggle for survival (Rizzini 1994).

2.3 Street Children's Survival Strategies

One of the most interesting and revealing aspects of existing research on street children concerns their daily life and how they survive in busy, violent and unfriendly urban environments. In Brazil, Columbia and India, children's accounts reveal how they earn their living; what their relations are with each other, police, and passers-by; what dangers they face; and what hopes they hold for future (Rizzini 1994, Knaul 1995, Patel 1990). The same studies have also noted that street children have been exploited in their work. Most children work long hours for poor wages. Children are not only exploited, but are exposed to many types of abuse, danger and violence, without the protection of labor laws. Experience from these countries documents that, while most of the children struggle to earn money by participating in culturally approved, income-generating activities, other children use less acceptable ways to make money. These activities, called "marginal" to distinguish them from legitimate work activities and to underscore the fact that they involve only a small percentage of children, can be divided into offences punishable by law (theft, robbery, prostitution, drug-pushing) and those not punishable by law (begging, vagrancy). In general, worldwide, street children engage in many activities in order to survive. They involve themselves in a host of remunerative activities such as vending, selling newspapers, cleaning cars, begging, shining shoes, pushing drugs and accepting work as parking boys.

Most people who work with street children, particularly law enforcement institutions, have difficulty understanding how the immediate pressing needs of street children influence the choices they make and the behavior they adopt. For example, many people consider the use of drugs by street children as very dangerous for their health. But the children themselves consider drugs a way of fighting hunger and fear and of making them carefree persons. As Diversi, *et al.* have argued, one serious consequence of this mismatch in perceptions of reality is that intervention programs have very often failed to address the needs of kids living on the streets (Diversi *et al.* 1999).

Most children become victims of violent acts exercised either by adults or by children themselves. Official child mortality rates in Brazilian cities indicate that homicide and suicide are the main causes of death among adolescents (IBGE 1989). A pioneering study on crimes committed against children on the streets of Rio de Janeiro, Sao Paulo and Recife discloses that 457 children were murdered between March and August 1989 (MNMMR *et. al.* 1991). These crimes, which resembled executions, are believed to have been committed by hired gun men. Suspects included drug traffickers; individuals who take justice into their own hands, commonly known

18

in Brazil as "vigilantes" (death or extermination squads); the military; civil police and private security guards (Rizzini 1994).

Preliminary studies in sub-Saharan Africa suggest that street children experience similar problems. Studies from Tanzania show that since most of these children hover on the periphery of other people's lives, some people classify them as problematic. The urban authorities see them as a menace to the city, thereby inflaming desires to see them eliminated from the urban environment. They are branded with pejoratives like "*wadokozi*" or "*wachomoaji*" (pick-pockets) or "*wahuni*" (hooligans) (Lugalla 1995b). According to section 176 of the Penal Code of Tanzania, street children are considered to be "Idle and Disorderly Persons" and are therefore regarded as criminals by government institutions (Lugalla 1995b). In most urban areas in Africa, street children are highly stigmatized, criminalized and demonized. In Kenya, they are labeled as "*Chokora-Mapipa.*" This means that they are the ones who depend on garbage and trash in order to survive. As Shorter and Onyancha (op.cit) have argued, "*Chokoraa*" is the material context of street children's daily life: "Like rubbish, he/she is to be thrown away". Society has no further use for him/her. He/she is non-person, someone who is not thought to have any rights, or even to be recognized by the law" (Shorter and Onyancha 1999).

Living independently at this young age makes them more vulnerable to and puts them at higher risk for both physical and sexual abuse. Cases of girls being raped and nonconsensual sodomy among boys are not hard to find. In their study "Sexual Experience of the Street Children of Mwanza in Tanzania," Rajani and Kudrati confirm that street children are particularly at risk for infection with HIV and other sexually transmitted diseases (STDs) for several reasons: the need to perform "survival sex" or prostitution, greater freedom to experiment with sex, and lack of adult protection and socialization (Kudrati and Rajani 1996). This study notes that sex plays a much larger and more central role in the lives of street girls than of boys, especially after puberty, and that the incidence and recurrence of STDs were also proportionately much higher in girls as compared to similarly physically mature boys. Eighty percent of the girls had STDs at least once, while 30% of boys were estimated to have experienced STDs during the same period. Street girls are prone to prostitution because they have a much a narrower range of options for earning a living. Under these circumstances, these girls lack assistance and alternative ways life and are forced to adopt survival behavior which is a risk to their health and reduces their self-esteem. In addition, they risk being beaten, experiencing rough sex, or going unpaid for sexual services they have rendered. Their suffering is both physical and psychological, and there is no doubt that in an era of rampant HIV/AIDS transmission, commercial sex as a survival strategy becomes a death strategy. These children also suffer from domestic, street-gang and drug-related violence.

2.4 How Countries Deal with the Problem

Many countries have adopted different strategies in order to address this problem. The kinds of attitudes and perceptions different government officials have about street children have tended to influence a great deal the kind of interventions that have been introduced. Negative attitudes have produced policies that address the symptoms rather than the real causes. And most of these policies have ended up hurting children rather than assisting them.

In countries like Brazil, the acute problems of street children have motivated the academic community to conduct research that has produced a new vision of street children. These studies have helped many in Brazil to change their attitudes about street children. There has been a shift away from a perception of them as social outcasts to a perception of them as victims of a social, economic and political system that puts them into the streets in order to survive or to help their families and themselves under very difficult economic circumstances (Blanc Szanton 1994). This knowledge has strengthened the children's rights and NGO movement in Brazil. This movement has been instrumental in initiating policy solutions that benefit these children.

Contrary to the conventional wisdom held by most government officials, NGO advocates in Brazil began insisting in late 1980s that street children working or living in streets were not a threat to society, nor were they without family or community ties. NGO activists brought their growing knowledge of the role of law, the Convention on the Right of the Child as well as their experiences of working with children in the streets. These developments added fresh yeast to the ferment in Brazil over serious violations of children's rights. As Donohue has argued in Blanc (1994), both the government and NGOs supported efforts on a small scale that began to bridge the gap between the world of work and the world of education. These efforts showed that educational training could assist, when used creatively, in bringing to a street child the type of education that strengthens his or her ability to earn more with greater dignity on the street. The objective of these efforts was to help children break out of dependency on street work and reinforce positive coping skills. Through these efforts, Brazilian society genuinely started to respond in new ways to long-standing problems experienced by street children. By listening to children, a change in mentality took place. Brazilian policy makers started realizing that street children could be a part of the solution, and adults, most of whom had negative attitudes towards these children,

20

were still a major part of the problem. Since then, a variety of policy programs have been established in order to ease the problem of street children.

What can countries of sub-Saharan Africa now experiencing a similar problem learn from the experience of working with street children in Brazil? Is the nature of the problem of street children in sub-Saharan Africa similar to or different from these other countries? Unlike in Asia, Latin and South America, why did countries in sub-Saharan Africa begin experiencing the problem of street children in mid 1980s and not before? What is unique to the African situation? How have the African family, social and economic structures changed over a period of time, and how are these structures contributing to the problem of street children? If Africa is unique in all these respects, what kind of unique policy solutions are required in order to deal with this social problem? Our study of street children in Tanzania is an attempt to address these issues.

2.5 Conclusion

The issue of street children is a global problem. Industrialized nations like the United States experience this problem as well as developing nations. However, as the data suggest, the magnitude of the problem is especially severe in developing countries due to poverty and social economic inequalities dominant in both rural and urban areas of these countries.

The children use a variety of survival tactics in order to cope with the hardships of urban life. Sometimes, they are forced to adopt illegal strategies that put them into conflict with law enforcement institutions. Although different countries are now beginning to address this problem, it is evident that the solutions being adopted tend to address symptoms of the problem rather than essential causes. This is because the problem is being analyzed outside the context of the very conditions that create it. In this study of street children in Tanzania, we have adopted a political economy approach in order to understand the essential relations behind this problem. Therefore, we begin chapter three with an analysis of the processes of social change, poverty and development that have taken place in Tanzania in order to examine the extent to which these changes have laid the foundation for the emergence of street children.

Chapter 3

Social Change, Urbanization and Poverty in Tanzania

3.1 Introduction

The United Republic of Tanzania, with a total population of 34.6 million (of which 33.6 million people are on the mainland part and the remaining in Zanzibar), is the largest country located in East Africa, covering 940,000 square kilometers, 60,000 of which is inland water (TDHS, 1990). In this study, Tanzania refers to the mainland part only. Tanzania lies South of the equator and borders eight countries. Kenya and Uganda are to the North; Democratic Republic of Congo, Rwanda and Burundi are to the West; Malawi and Mozambique are to the South and Zambia is to the Southwest (ibid). The main climate feature for most parts of the country is the long dry spell from May to October, followed by a period of rainfall from November to April. The main rainy season along the coast and the area around Mount Kilimanjaro is from March to May with short rains between October and December. In the western part of the country around Lake Victoria, rainfall is well distributed throughout the year with the peak period between March and May (ibid).

Tanzania was a German colony between 1884-1917. During this time, it was called German East Africa. After World War I, the British, who changed the name to Tanganyika, colonized the country. Tanganyika got her independence December 9, 1961 and it became a republic a year later. April 26, 1964, Tanganyika united with Zanzibar and formed the United Republic of Tanzania. By then, Zanzibar had just become independent after overthrowing the rule of the Sultanate on January 12, 1964. Tanzania's mainland is divided into 21 regions and Zanzibar's into 5 regions. Each region is subdivided into districts, which are in turn divided into divisions, wards and villages.

The country has undergone a variety of processes of social, political, cultural and economic changes since colonization. Much of what has characterized Tanzania today is a product of these processes. Therefore, in order to understand the contemporary problems that Tanzania is facing, a historical analysis of these processes is important.

The purpose of this chapter is to examine some processes of the social change and development of the Tanzanian mainland and to assess how those processes have enhanced poverty and urbanization. Our interest is in the extent to which these historical processes of social change have ended up creating an environment that has been capable of manufacturing helpless street children. We begin this analysis by presenting in brief the economic situation of Tanzania.

3.2 Tanzania's Current Economic Situation

Tanzania is one of the poorest countries in the world. According to the World Development Report of 1997, Tanzania has the third lowest GNP per capita in the world-$120 (Narayan, 1997). Although this figure may underestimate the actual national income and patterns of expenditure, it is estimated that a minimum of 30% of the total GNP takes place in the second economy (Narayan 1997). According to Narayan, the activities of the second economy include production and sale of goods and services from the informal sector and barter transactions that are not captured by official accounting and taxation systems. Rent-seeking activities and illicit activities such as traffic in exports and narcotics are examples. If these activities were included in official income statistics, they would probably raise the national income by between 40 and 50% (Maliyamkono and Bagachwa 1990, World Bank 1994, Narayan 1997).

According to a 1997 World Bank study, approximately one half of the population lives at very low levels of welfare (Narayan, 1997). As of 1991, about one half of the rural population was living in poverty with 42% of all rural Tanzanians in extreme poverty (Ibid). According to Ferreira and Griffin, the average per person consumption expenditure in 1993-94 in rural areas was 50 cents a day.

Although areas designated as urban are increasing along with the urban population and the growing number of impoverished people living in urban areas, poverty in Tanzania is still a predominately rural phenomenon. The majority of Tanzanians (approximately 80%) live in the rural areas where they survive by practicing subsistence farming. Most farming is traditional; land–intensive, low–input, subsistence agriculture. Although agriculture production has been increasing during the last few years, production output from this sector continues to be low and have stagnated fro almost three decades. And according to the recent Household Budget Survey, the rural small holder farmers are five times more likely to be poor than those who receive a wage from the public or private sector precisely because of the underdeveloped environment within which rural economic production takes place. About 87% of the Tanzanian poor live in rural areas (HBS 2002). The Tanzanian population continues to be largely dependent on agriculture, but non-agricultural activities have become increasingly important since the early 1990s. Manufacturing contributes a mere 7 percent of GDP. Privatization of state-owned institutions and policies that promote retrenchment of workers have led to a decline in government and parastatal employment and a significant rise in private sector and self-employment activities. These and the informal sector have grown considerably since the government adopted the prescription for economic crises from the Bretton Woods institutions. Since this prescription, there is a limited uptake of banking and involvement in other savings facilities, particularly in rural areas. The participation of poor people in informal savings groups has declined over the 1990s (HBS 2002). Most likely, it is because the majority of people have been structurally adjusted to the extent that they have nothing to bank or save. Most of the rural people are poor because rural areas of Tanzania are inherently underdeveloped, and the dominant form of agricultural production is geared towards exports. Other major economic activities include food processing and manufacturing building materials, paper and packaging largely for the internal market. Tanzania 's exports consisting of agricultural products and materials have hardly improved or been diversified since the early 1980's. Although the country's population is predominantly rural, its urban population is growing at about 5 percent annually. The six largest cities generate over one third of the GDP with Dar-es-Salaam accounting for 17 percent (World Development Report 1999/2000). This notwithstanding, Tanzania cities continue to be parasitic to their rural hinterlands. They continue to depend on surplus produced from the countryside for their survival- a situation that further under develops the rural areas. Why are these places inherently poor and underdeveloped is question that cannot be answered outside the analysis of processes of social change and development that have taken place in Tanzania from colonialism to date.

3.3 Colonialism and Rural Underdevelopment

Tanzania became a German colony after the 1884 Berlin Conference's scrambling and partitioning of Africa. In 1918, after World War I, Tanzania was placed under the British Mandate and remained a trusteeship territory of the leagues of Nations until it achieved independence in 1961. The Germans ruled Tanzania for 30 years, and the British ruled for 45 years. In both periods, the economy of Tanzania was designed in such a way that it had to fulfill the objectives of the colonial interests. The colonial economy introduced the production of raw materials, agricultural cash crops like coffee, tea, sisal, tobacco, cotton and others, through both settler and peasant mixed farming.

The Germans used three main ways of organizing their economy: white settler farming, plantation farming operated by foreign companies, and small-scale peasant cash-crop production (Lugalla, 1995). Setting the colonial economy in motion necessarily involved a "redirecting" of the means of production so that they could suit colonial interests and demands. The most affected were the pre-colonial social structure, land and labor (Ibid). Fertile land was alienated from local Tanzanians in order to pave the way for plantation and estate farming. The colonial state introduced the money economy (money as the medium of exchange) and in 1897, imposed taxation that was to be paid in money form. The colonial state also demarcated areas

24

for production of exports and areas for supplying labor to the plantation economy (labor reserves). For example, Njombe, Songea, Rukwa and Kigoma were supposed to provide migrant labor to sugar and sisal plantations in the Morogoro and Tanga regions.

As a result of these colonial economic strategies, many Tanzanians lost their fertile agricultural land. Additionally, many of them began producing cash crops (crops they had never consumed), and even worse some of them did so at the expense of the production of their food. Those who lost land or lived in labor reserves had to migrate to other rural areas to seek employment in export-crop plantation; others migrated to the urban areas to look for jobs in the colonial state bureaucracy. Due to colonial interests, Africans began, for the first time, to migrate from rural areas in search of economic opportunities elsewhere. Job opportunities in the colonial state bureaucracy required Africans to have a minimal education. In order to achieve this end, the colonial state introduced its own system of education, which prepared Africans for urban-based, white-collar jobs. The curriculum of education was alien and very irrelevant; it in no way addressed the local problems and needs of Tanzanians.

Of central importance to the colonial economy was infrastructure for communication, commerce and administration. The colonial state built telephone lines, roads, and railway lines in order to link export-crop-producing rural areas with the port. In fact, until the Chinese built the Tanzania-Zambia railway line (TAZARA), Tanzania's railway system was essentially what the Germans left behind.

The pattern of communication infrastructure was determined by economic considerations. The communication network was outward oriented. It was not built to promote the internal domestic market, but rather to make sure that the raw materials produced in Tanzania could easily find their way out to Europe. Having a road network that aspired to build an internal self-sustaining economy was not the goal of the colonial economy. While all regional areas that were favorable for cash crop production became easily accessible by railway and road systems, the southern parts of Tanzania remained inaccessible because they were not profitable to the colonial economy. In addition to communication infrastructure, the colonial state established centers of commerce and administration in order to supervise the colonial economy. Most of the cities and towns in Tanzania emerged as a result of these moves. The urban areas were never meant to be centers of production. They were service oriented, and their survival depended on surplus produced from the countryside. Unfortunately, this infrastructure has, to a very considerable extent, continued to run along the lines laid out by colonial politics. When the British took over Tanganyika, they did not alter what the Germans had already laid down. This is clearly noted from the statement in 1926 from the British Governor, Sir Donald Cameron, who said that,

"The first objective of the government is to induce the native to become a producer directly or indirectly, that is to produce or to assist in producing something more than the crop of local foodstuffs that he requires for himself and his family"(Coulson, 1982).

This means that the structure of the economy remained the same and emphasis on cash-crop production continued unabated. From the mid 1930s to the mid 1950s, the British believed that force was necessary to make rural farmers change their agricultural techniques. They amended the Native Authorities Ordinance in 1937 in order to allow by-laws to be passed for enforcement of soil conservation measures and other agricultural practices (ibid.).

By the time Tanzania achieved independence, the colonial politics had established strong roots for an outside-oriented economy in rural Tanzania. These politics led to an underdeveloped rural Tanzania in a variety of ways. By redirecting the Africans from farming for subsistence to cash crop production, Tanzanian farmers became dependent on the forces and dictates of the international capitalist system outside their own will. Unfortunately, rural farmers of Tanzania have, up until now, not been able to opt out of the web of capitalist production. By introducing policies that encouraged and fostered rural differentiation, colonial economic policies divided the rural people into rich, poor and middle peasants. These policies also enhanced unequal regional development. By introducing an economy that does not serve the internal markets, colonialism initiated a systematic process of rural surplus appropriation. It is this process that has continued to enhance the social relations of poverty and underdevelopment not only in rural areas, but also in urban areas. Surplus that is produced in the rural areas is not used to promote social progress in rural areas; rather, it is partly invested in funding luxurious service structures in urban areas, and the rest is whisked outside the country (Lugalla 1995). In general, the colonial economy had an adverse impact on Tanzania's social economic structure. It created a wide gap between the rural and urban areas and created special urban forms that perform specific functions. The cities and towns that were established became parasitic rather than generative in relation to their rural hinterlands. The process of rural-urban migration was very insignificant during colonialism because the colonial state established strict laws restricting African urban migration. One such law, the Colonial Labor Utilization Ordinance of 1923, regulated the movement of native Africans from villages to urban areas. It also made it possible for the government to account for all blacks living in urban areas and to repatriate any of those not working to the rural areas (Lugalla 1997). The place for the Africans was the countryside; very few of them were allowed to live in urban areas so that they could supply cheap labor to the European-owned businesses and the colonial government (ibid).

It is against this background that the nature of urbanization, rural underdevelopment, rural poverty and rural-urban migration in Tanzania has to be understood. In the section that follows we will address the question of whether or not post-colonial state policies of social change and development altered the legacy of colonialism.

3.4 Post-Colonial State Development Policies

Tanzania achieved independence in December 1961. Since then, the post-colonial states have been adopting a variety of policy measures in order to transform the social economic situation of Tanzania. We can divide the post-colonial period into three main periods. The first period covers the first six years of independence. The second period begins with 1967 and ends in mid 1980s. This is considered as the period of socialist construction and the beginning of the social economic crisis. The third period begins in 1986 and extends into the present. We have labeled this the period of economic crisis and Structural Adjustment. In the sections that follow, we examine each period separately in order to understand the policies that dominated each period, and how these policies produced conditions that tend to generate the rapid growth of street children in Tanzania.

i) The Period after Independence (1961-1966)

As we have demonstrated above, the colonial heritage of Tanzania was the backdrop against which its existence as a newly independent country developed. During the first few years of independence, the ruling party TANU (Tanganyika African National Union) spent much time consolidating the independence and Africanizing the post-colonial state bureaucracy. There was no massive effort to transform radically the social economic relations that the new state inherited from colonialism. The country strove to speed up the growth rate of the economy by welcoming aid and private investment from Western capitalist countries and particularly Great Britain (the former colonial master). Tanzania maintained good relations with the United Kingdom and continued to depend on the crown to finance the first three-year and first five-year development plans. Whether this was deliberate or not, it is difficult to tell, but there is every reason to believe that the leaders of the post-colonial state did not know the relationship between finance capitalism, colonialism and neo-colonialism.

The few major social changes introduced during this period were the use of Kiswahili as the national language, the abolition of traditional chiefdoms, and the introduction of a one party political system. As opposed to colonial politics, the post-colonial state also relaxed the strict regulations of rural-urban migration and discriminative policies that existed during colonialism. The agricultural policy as well as urban development policies that had been introduced by the colonial government continued to operate unabated.

The cities and towns continued to grow and perform the same roles that had been laid down by the colonial state. However, because of relaxing the laws against rural-urban migration, the rate of Africans drifting from rural to urban areas increased, resulting in rapid growth of the urban African population. For example, from 1948-57, the rate of growth of the population of Dar-es-Salaam increased by 9% every year, but shot up to 14% from 1961-67 (Lugalla 1997). High rates of growth for the African and predominantly low-income populations were also notable in other smaller towns (Lugalla 1995). But since the cities and towns were predominantly administrative centers and did not generate their own surplus, they were not capable of absorbing the surplus labor force now flocking to urban areas. Hence, problems of unemployment intensified, and urban conditions of squalor and poverty were greatly exacerbated.

ii) The Era of Socialist Construction (1967-1980)

Tanzania introduced major political changes in 1967. President Nyerere and his ruling party announced the Arusha Declaration on February 5, 1967. The declaration was considered a blueprint for socialist construction. The Arusha Declaration rejected capitalism as an appropriate path of development for Tanzania. It also rejected exploitation of human beings and all forms of social inequality. The declaration vowed to build a socialist society based on the principles of the traditional African family (Ujamaa). The Ujamaa policy, which focused on rural development and self-reliance, introduced free education and medical care. The government nationalized schools, health institutions, and the so-called commanding heights of the economy, such as land, banks, insurance companies and other large industries. In order to control the entire economy, the government established a variety of public companies (parastatals) to deal with some productive and service activities of the economy. In order to promote rural development, forced measures of putting people into Ujamaa/Development villages were implemented. Schools and health centers were opened in almost every village. And attempts were made by the government to make sure that reliable and clean water was available to the majority rural population. In 1975, the government introduced the policy of Universal Primary Education (UPE) to assure that every child who was old enough to be in school had a chance to be there.

28

The government also began—albeit slowly—to decolonize the system of education in Tanzania, particularly in primary schools.

The first ten years of socialist construction showed a great deal of social progress. Rural areas began to change, and many children were enrolled in primary and secondary schools. Between 1974 and 1978, the number of children enrolled in Standard One increased by 254%, from 248,000 to 878,321 pupils. Overall enrollment in primary schools rose from 1,228,886 in 1974 to a proportional peak of 3,553,144 in 1983 (MOEC 1998, Kuleana 1999). At the height of the UPE drive, Tanzania achieved a gross enrollment ration of 98% for primary education, and the gender differences that existed in primary education were virtually eliminated (ibid). Accessibility to health care improved, and many rural people began getting reliable sources of clean water. The Ujamaa policy, despite its failure to create a socialist mecca, managed to introduce human-oriented policies emphasizing redistribution of economic growth to the rural poor. The education and health infrastructure was improved in rural areas, and the majority of the people were forced to live first in Ujamaa villages and later in development villages. Although the policy was coercive and sometimes violated some basic principles of human rights, it, nevertheless, created conditions allowing the majority rural poor access to such basic resources as land for agricultural development and social services. The policies discouraged rural-urban migration, and therefore limited the growth of the population of street children during this period.

While the "Ujamaa" policies had a positive impact on the welfare of the majority of the rural population, their ad-hoc and poor implementation by some leaders created some problems, laying the foundation of the economic crisis that Tanzania began to experience from the late 1970s to mid 1980s (the second 10 years of socialist construction). Ultimately, this forced Tanzania to adopt the policies of structural adjustment.

iii) The Era of Economic Crisis and Structural Adjustments (SAPS) 1986-2002

According to Kipokola (1998), SAPs in sub-Saharan Africa may be generalized to represent belated macro economic management responses to the situations of excessive policy and structural distortions built up over a number of years, especially from the late 1970s onward. The causal factors for economic deterioration vary from country to country, but in all cases, both internal and external factors have been at play (Kipokola, 1998). In Tanzania, there were many factors that sparked the crisis during the late 1970s. The policy of socialism, which shifted emphasis to public ownership of property and increased the role of the government and government intervention in economic activity, contributed to the crisis by creating a bloated

29

government bureaucracy that was predominantly engaged in redistributing services rather than in productive activities. This situation, coupled with external factors such as the oil price shocks (1973-74 and 1979-80), the collapse of the East African Community (1977), the 1978 coffee boom with its sudden price collapse and the war with Uganda (1978-79) created severe economic instability in Tanzania in the late 1970s (ibid).

Tanzania's social economic crisis manifested itself in extensive and persistent internal and external macroeconomic imbalances. The internal disequilibria were evident mainly in growing savings-investment gaps at a time when government expenditure was growing. Agricultural production declined, leading to a shortage of foreign earnings. This shortage of foreign earnings made it difficult for the government to import manufactured goods from abroad, such as fuel and industrial spare parts, in turn, paralyzing the industrial sector and resulting in a progressive decline in industrial capacity utilization. Acute shortages of basic essential commodities like clothing, sugar, soap and cooking oil resulted. Existing data also demonstrate that real agriculture output declined. The only sector that continued to expand in real terms was public administration and other services (Lipumba 1984). The fundamental political economy problem of Tanzania at this time was that material production was decreasing, but public administration was expanding. In Marxist terms, one would say that the superstructure had become a fetter to the development of productive forces. Such growth increased the burden of the government at a time when the government was experiencing financial resource constraints. As a consequence, the government failed to finance or maintain the service infrastructure, as well as its bloated bureaucracy. The quality of services such as health and education also deteriorated tremendously. Scarcity of essential commodities became the norm, a fact that encouraged hoarding, black-marketeering, and corruption. Attempts by the government to introduce a rationing system for the scarce essential items also ended up creating new contradictions. Long waiting lines resulted, first in offices to obtain permits and then at the distribution point of these commodities (Lipumba 1984).

The net result of this crisis has been two-fold: first, there was a deterioration of the standard of living of the majority of the people in both rural and urban areas on the one hand, and there was an erosion of the social and economic development that was achieved during the first fifteen years of independence on the other.

In order to improve the situation, Tanzania signed an agreement with the World Bank in 1986 and adopted the structural adjustment policies (SAPs). These policies seek to attain macro-economic balance by bringing national expenditure into line with national income. They advocate devaluation of the local currency, privatization, liberalization of the entire economy, retrenchment of workers, and the introduction of user fees in social services like health and education. SAPs have had different effects on different social groups. A variety of studies have noted already that SAPs have been extremely detrimental to the life conditions of the majority poor (Lugalla 1995 and 1997, Mlawa and Green 1998). The devaluation of the local currency has been responsible for pushing up prices of both locally produced and imported commodities. Reduction of government expenditures has had disastrous effects on the provision of social services and on the availability of employment opportunities in the public sector. Policies advocating the privatization of parastatals and retrenchment of workers have ended up raising the number of unemployed people. The abolition of government subsidies on agricultural inputs like fertilizer and better seeds has pushed up the cost of production in the agricultural sector, which has, in turn, increased the prices of agricultural products and, in particular, the prices of foodstuffs in urban areas. Although the government has been raising the minimum wage since 1980, this raise has never matched the rapidly rising cost of living that has been occurring during the SAP period. The net result of the stagnation of real wages and of galloping inflation for the majority of people is that they have suffered great erosion in their purchasing power. This has been happening at a time in which people are supposed to pay for the cost of their health and the education of their children. This situation has forced many people to moonlight and to adopt a variety of legal, illegal, moral and immoral coping strategies.

SAPS have brought a lot of changes, not only at macro level where policies are implemented, but also more significantly at the micro household level where women are most affected (Lugalla 1995ab). They have shifted the national burdens to the poor through inflation and rising costs of basic necessities (Farmer et al. 1996). As Farmer and others argue, in most cities in Africa, people who used to eat three meals a day have been forced to adjust to either a single meal or to skip food for days (ibid).

A study by Lugalla shows that SAPS have created classes of the "new poor" and "chronic poor" and that the majority poor continue to be marginalized by powerful forces beyond their control (Lugalla 1997). In these times, poor women bear the brunt of increased workloads, declining incomes and increased sickness. Women are now forced to work harder and longer within the market and also in the domestic household economy in order to supplement rapidly declining family incomes. For some women, sexual patron-client relations and multiple partner strategies that supplement their incomes have become increasingly important means of survival. At the same time, competition among the self-employed is intense, and many women remain impoverished despite long hours of arduous labor. If their income-generating projects fail, some of them end up supplementing their incomes by trading sexual

31

services (prostitution)—a survival strategy that has now turned into a death strategy due to AIDS. Gender inequality and poverty rob women of their ability to fulfill their socially designated responsibilities and thus, debase them, often forcing them into prostitution.

Although our analysis demonstrates that the impact of globalization and SAPs is negative, the Bretton Woods institutions and the World Trade Organization (WTO) hold a different view. According to these institutions, SAPs are working and, globalization is bearing healthy fruit. Taking Tanzania as a success story, they argue that SAPs have brought inflation down to below 7% and that the GNP is growing at a rate of 4% per year. They cite sedans and SUVs that glide in the streets of major cities, shops that are filled with imported goods and report that mining and cash crops exports are up (*Time Magazine* April 24, 2000). In absolute terms, poverty increased over the 1990s. There are now 11.4 million Tanzanians below the basic needs line compared with 9.5 million in 1991-92 (Household Budget Survey [HBS] 2002). These men and women, who are mostly subsistence or small-plot cash-crop farmers, have been structurally adjusted half to death (ibid). Devaluation and elimination of agricultural subsidies double and quadruple agricultural inputs like fertilizer while famine remains a persistent threat for 40% of the population (ibid). With a foreign loan of 6.4 billion, the current government has been spending 40% of its annual revenue on interest payments. This is more than what it spends on health and education combined. Even the poorest families are subjected to cost-sharing in health and education. As far as health is concerned, this has now forced approximately 70% of the people to consult faith or traditional healers. Due to cost-sharing policies, when they are ill, the poor are less likely to see a health provider, whether private or public. The great misfortune here is that this is happening in a country with a serious AIDS epidemic.

As if the social economic crisis was not enough, the AIDS epidemic that has invaded the country during the same period has also increased the burden of many Tanzanian families. The economic crisis, increasing poverty and the AIDS epidemic have destroyed families, communities and other traditional systems of social support that have existed in extended families. Young parents are dying due to HIV/AIDS, leaving behind helpless, orphaned children--some of whom are also HIV positive. The life of such children is difficult, very short and very painful. The increasing situation of poverty for the majority of the people has intensified the already existing gender inequality by enhancing economic dependence of women on men. A variety of studies have already documented that poor women are more likely to be less powerful in negotiating sexual encounters and tend to be more vulnerable to high-risk sexual relationships because of economic dependence (Schoepf 1996, Lugalla 1999). The

32

dire need to survive and feed their families has forced a larger number of Tanzanian women to practice survival sex (Lugalla 1999). The increasing number of "*Changu-Doas*"(prostitutes) in most urban areas of Tanzania is a case in point. This situation is not only creating young, immature mothers and putting women in a vulnerable situations regarding HIV infection, it is also leading to the production of an increasing number of fatherless children. During the current period of crisis, women and children's labor is heavily pressed and harnessed. The payment of user fees in education is deterring many parents from enrolling their children in schools, particularly girls. At the same time, due to rampant gender inequality, women in rural areas do not have access to property and resources of wealth and power. The net result of all this is that an increasing number of young women are escaping rural drudgery by migrating to the city in search of low paying jobs in the informal sector. Some women who fail to get employment in this sector are more likely to be involved in survival sex. A study by Mpangile *et al.*, (1993) has noted the rampant existence of old rich men ("sugar daddies") in urban areas who lure young girls with money and luxurious lifestyles in exchange for sex. Looking at these changes, there is ample reason to believe that there is a very close association between the increasing situation of poverty, rural-urban migration and the rapid spread of HIV/AIDS.

As will be demonstrated in the next chapter, as a result of poverty and hardships experienced in rural areas, many youth and young children have increasingly been migrating to urban areas in search of an alternative way of life. Unlike Kenya, where the phenomenon of street children has been dominant since independence, for Tanzania, the problem of street children is a recent phenomenon. The problem developed into alarming proportions during the period of crisis and structural adjustments. There is no doubt, therefore, that the processes of social change and development that have been brought by the economic crisis and that the policies of structural adjustment must be creating conditions that generate massive numbers of street children. It is also important to examine how these processes of social change and development associated with economic crisis and structural adjustments are impacting processes and institutions of socializing children. In order to do so, we examine the changing nature of the African family and its ways of socializing children. We then look at how the economic crisis and SAPs have destroyed the present quality of education of Tanzania.

3.5 Conclusion

This chapter has attempted to present parameters for understanding the nature of the political economy of Tanzania. We have examined in brief policies and processes of social change and development that have been happening in Tanzania from the period of colonialism to the present, and how these processes have been responsible for creating specific conditions in rural and urban areas. We are now aware of how the situation of dependency and underdevelopment was introduced during colonialism, maintained and perpetuated by post-colonial policies. There is clear evidence that the economic crisis that Tanzania has been experiencing has been caused by both internal and external factors. Together with the economic crisis, the policies of structural adjustment that Tanzania has adopted in order to address its economic ills have created new contradictions. Poverty has intensified in both rural and urban areas. The 2001 Household Budget Survey confirms that income poverty is high and that many social indicators are poor in Tanzania. The increasing situation of poverty has destroyed families and communities and has ended up putting women and children in vulnerable conditions. This chapter is important because it has set a concrete historical background that assists us in understanding the nature of social relations of poverty in Tanzania. It is these relations that can help us to understand why Tanzania began experiencing a serious problem regarding unsupervised children living alone in urban streets in mid 1980s and early 1990s. We strongly believe that the problem of street children in Tanzania can only be fully understood if the analysis of its development is situated within the context of Tanzania's political economy. Our discussion of the nature of street children of Tanzania, the hardship and violence they experience in urban areas and the implications for their health can only be understood within this perspective.

Chapter 4

The Nature of Street Children in Tanzania

4.1 Introduction

In this chapter, we present the main findings of this study. We begin by examining the nature of the street children who were included in our study population. Our main focus is on exploring the factors that have pushed them out of their families, their methods of survival in an urban setting, the nature of these settings and how street children adopt to this environment, and how they try to make use of it in order to survive. Our main argument is that street children live in a different social environment compared to other children in the larger society. While in this different social environment, street children learn different ways of life, most of which reflect the difficulties associated with urban life in poor societies. The street children are forced to develop different sets of skills that assist them in surviving in an urban environment. Children's interactions in daily behavior settings shape not only their economic activities and life styles, but also their socialization, interpersonal relationships, and general cognitive and perceptual functioning and development (Shinha 1982, Verma 1999). As Verma (1999) has argued, we can expect that street children will be socialized to learn the roles, competencies, and adaptive skills ranging from those needed for self-preservation and economic survival to more fundamental, interpersonal and cognitive ones.

We begin this analysis by describing, in the section below, the social demographic characteristics of the street children of the city Dar-es-Salaam, who were included in our study population.

4.2 The Socio-Demographic Characteristics

Our study population involved a total of 403 street children. Three hundred and fifty two, or 87.03%, were street boys and only 51, or 12.7%, were street girls.

Figure 3: Street Children Interviewed by Sex and Percentages

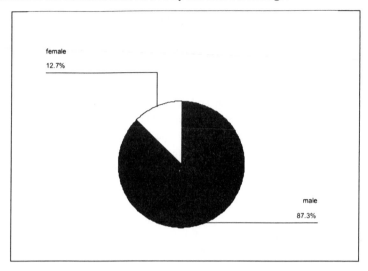

Forty-four percent were Christians and 54% were Moslems. The reasons for recruiting fewer street girls are obvious. In most cities of sub-Saharan Africa, street girls tend to be less visible than street boys for a number of reasons. This does not mean that girls are less affected by factors that push children to streets. But their invisibility is very much the result of a variety of cultural forces. Traditionally, most cultures in Tanzania tend to exercise more control over girls than over boys. Tanzanian families define the home and the domestic sphere of life as the domain of girls. To the contrary, boys are supposed to be active in the public sphere of life, which means outside the home. Due to this, girls are given many domestic responsibilities, which tend to hinder them from free movement. If they succeed in leaving their homes and are on their own in the streets, they tend to hide themselves out of fear of sexual harassment and molestation. This scenario has also been observed in other countries. A study in Kenya noted that male street children greatly outnumbered female street children (Aptekar et al. 1999). The study found that most Kenyan boys were taught by their impoverished head-of-household mothers to cope with a very limited economic environment by becoming independent at a far earlier age than the dominant society deemed appropriate (Aptekar et al. 1995, Aptekar and Stocklin 1996, Aptekar et al. 1999). The study also noted that Kenyan mothers taught girls to cope with the difficulties of poverty by staying at home. Thus, if poor girls

36

became street girls, their presence on the street stemmed from a breakdown in the family process.

At the same time, it is important to note the influence of labor market structures in the gender differences of street children. Most opportunities for labor in Tanzania are biased against girls/women. Men/boys have a greater variety of employment opportunities than girls. This means that in a situation of difficulties at home, boys are more likely to leave their homes at an earlier age than girls, with a hope that things might get better in the outside sphere of the domestic household economy. At the same time, most people tend to have negative attitudes towards girls who are seen roaming aimlessly in urban street. We also need to mention arranged marriages for girls, which usually occur at an early stage. All of these factors explain why the number of street girls is lower than that of boys. Most of the girls operate as prostitutes at night. Some of them are hired as domestic servants once they arrive in an urban setting; therefore, they are kept indoors most of the time. Men or pimps, who provide them with housing and security in exchange for sexual favors, easily take some and hide them in their homes or guesthouses. These factors render them invisible during the daytime.

Tanzanian children become street children at a very tender age. About two thirds (60%) of the street children we interviewed were between 11 and 16 years of age. The same trend was observed when age of street children was analyzed by sex (Table 1).

37

Table 1: Street Children Interviewed by Age and Sex

Age Group	Boys	%	Girls	%	Boys & Girls	Total %
5-8	7	2	1	2	8	2.0
9-10	24	6.8	2	3.9	26	6.5
11-13	74	21	6	11.8	80	19.9
14-16	136	38.6	28	54.9	164	40.8
>16	85	24.1	12	23.5	97	24.1
Don't know	14	4.0	1	2	15	3.7
Missing	12	3.4	1	2	13	3.0
TOTAL	352	100.0	51	100.0	403	100.0

Source: Research Findings.

Why do most children resort to street life at this tender age? There are a variety of possible reasons. First and foremost is the fact that most children graduate from primary schools at this age. Second, it is at this age that children from poor families are more likely to be sent out to work or to be required to help their parents to supplement family income by being involved in petty income generating activities. Third, this is a delicate age for most children. For boys approaching adolescence, this is the time when they start asserting their own self and sexual identity. This can lead to conflict in the family or to children's refusal to tolerate the difficult circumstances at home. Fourth, severe conflicts are likely to happen between the behavioral expectations of conservative parents and the new ways of life associated with the winds of modernization that are currently sweeping across cities of sub-Saharan Africa.

Information on education reveals that most children are not graduates of primary schools. Most of them have either dropped out of school or have never attended school. Of the 352 boys, only 17% had completed Standard Seven primary education. About a third had never attended school and 51% had dropped out of school. As for the girls, a third (33%) had never attended school, only 12% managed to complete

38

primary school and more than half (53%) stated that they had dropped out of school. A third of the boys (31%) dropped out of school when they were between the first and fourth grade and 19% dropped out when they were between fifth and seventh grade. The drop out rates for girls is almost the same between those who dropped out between first and fourth and between fifth and seventh grades. Overall, for both sexes, most street children dropped out of school when they were still in lower primary or elementary schools (first and fourth grade).

In terms of reasons for dropping out of the school, the overall response for both boys and girls reveals that poverty-related reasons predominate (24%), followed by lack of interest and motivation (8.2%), child abuse (6.7%), and lack of interest together with child abuse (7.7%). By poverty-related reasons, we mean the inability of the family to buy school uniforms, books, stationary, or to pay the fees. By child abuse, we mean harassment at home or school, sexual abuse, battering and any other physical harm inflicted by adults on children--a harm that affects the child psychologically and forces him or her to leave home and school. These findings do not differ with the data recorded by the Household Budget Survey of Tanzania in 2002. This survey revealed that 12% of the respondents stated that the cost of education was the main reason for dropping out or not attending school; 10% of them said that school was useless and uninteresting and 9% were absent due to work (HBS 2002).

In-depth interviews reveal the reasons for dropping out of school: lack of uniforms, failure to pay school fees, inability to buy books and stationary, and severe physical punishment at school. Some girls cited sexual harassment, pregnancy and running away from home in fear of early arranged marriages. The school environment also plays an important role in making children less interested in school. Our focus group discussions recorded many complaints about overcrowded classes, no desks, lack of teachers and essential equipment like books, maps, visual aids and sanitary facilities. All these problems, when accompanied by poverty and a hard life at home, tend to make students think that success in life lies elsewhere, outside of school. Our findings indicate that street children were rarely expelled from school, due to lack of appropriate discipline.

In general, the analysis stemming from these findings shows that poverty and abuse tend to increase the number of school dropouts. As we have already argued in the previous chapter, the persistently rising situation of poverty is inevitably linked to the social economic crisis and the impact of structural adjustment policies. The introduction of cost-sharing policies in education means that Tanzanian parents are currently supposed to pay for the education of their children. Although, by law, parents are supposed to pay only 2000 Tanzanian shilling (Tshs.) per child per year

($2.50), many parents have many children in different schools and can hardly afford it. At the same time, there are other forms of compulsory payments or "contributions" (to use the polite terminology) for buildings, desks, political rallies, i.e. "*Mbio za Mwenge wa Uhuru*" (Uhuru-Independence Torch Race). When expenses for books, uniforms and stationary are added to overhead costs, most parents become overburdened with financial liability and end up opting to withdraw their children from schooling.

Many boys stated that their families were large with many children who were supposed to be in school. They had to drop out because their parents could not afford it. Some girls told us their parents did not take them to school because they were spending their meager resources in educating their brothers. Two sisters responded to us in the following way:

> "My sister and I left our village in order to come to Dar-es-Salaam to look for work. Our father told us that he only had money to educate our brothers. When we arrived in Dar-es-Salaam, an unknown woman picked us at the Tanzania Zambia Railway station (TAZARA) and employed us as domestic servants. We ran away from her because she was very abusive."

The above narrative requires some qualifications. Besides domestic responsibility and early marriages, many conservative rural parents prefer spending their meager resources in educating boys rather than girls. The belief that a woman's place is the home and that boys have a special value in society to act as life insurance for parents in their old age, tend to greatly influence these decisions. Due to poverty, mortgaging the future of their children for their own benefit remains the only alternative.

The picture of these reasons changes if one looks at them along gender lines. While the boys stated poverty-related reasons as factors that forced them to drop out of school, 18% of the girls mentioned abuse, 16% cited poverty-related reasons and 14% stated lack of interest and motivation.

Besides being very young, lack of appropriate education makes it difficult for street children to possess socially accepted skills. This is evidenced by their response to our question of "Whether they possessed socially approved skills". By socially approved skills, we meant skills that enabled children to engage in socially approved activities like vending, car washing, working as parking boys, shoe shining, and others. We did not consider pick pocketing, begging, garbage picking, transport vehicle barking (*wapiga debe*), and prostitution to be socially approved activities.

Only 50 boys (12.4%) and 8 girls (16%) had socially approved skills that allowed them work in the socially approved activities of the informal sector such as vending, shoe-shining and social-service-related activities. Of the 352 boys, 306, or more than four fifths (87%), did not possess any socially approved skill. About 80% of the girls also belonged to this category.

4.3 The Street Children's Family Background

Our findings reveal that most street children come from poor families (81%). Only 17% stated that they came from middle class families.

Figure 4: Economic Status of Families of Street Children

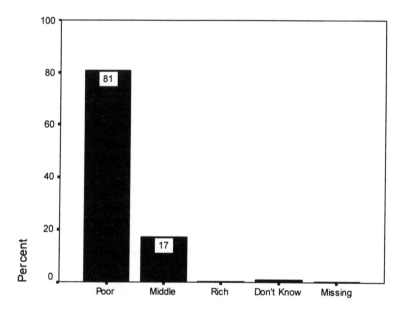

Economic Status of Family

In terms of sex, 82% of the boys and 77% of the girls came from poor families. In most Tanzanian societies, housing conditions and their surroundings tend to reflect the social as well as the economic status of the household. Different social classes live in different houses, and these houses differ in terms of area, location, size, building materials, sanitary systems and level of overcrowding per household. One can therefore use the variable of housing in order to understand the nature of society's social structure. In order to understand more about the characteristics of poverty, we asked the children to describe their parents' homes. Two thirds came from houses made of mud with thatched roofs. This is typical housing for most of the rural poor in Tanzania. Close to a half of the children came from larger families of between 6-10 members. More than a third came from single parents, of which 73 (18.1%) and 63 (15.6%) had mothers and fathers respectively. For both sexes, children with single parents tended to stay with their mothers rather than their fathers. Certainly, this is a reflection of the role of a Tanzanian woman in a Tanzanian family. Thirty-one percent came from married monogamous families. The remaining third came from unmarried monogamous families (7.4%), married polygamous families (9.9%), unmarried polygamous families (2.5%), and 15% were orphans.

We categorized orphans as those who have lost both parents, but in-depth interviews showed that most of those staying with a single parent (122 out of 136) had lost the other parent due to death. This means that if we define an orphan as one who has lost one or both parents, about 181 (44.9%) were orphans. A recent study in the Ileje district on rural-based street children has also observed a close association between the increasing number of orphaned children and the increasing number of street children (Lugalla and Barongo 2000). Although it is difficult for us to argue affirmatively why many street children are orphans, one can associate these deaths with the HIV/AIDS epidemic that has currently swept the entire country, rural and urban areas alike. Our research findings suggest that most of the street children are sons and daughters of parents who have hardly attended beyond primary education. Although more than one third did not know the education level achieved by their parents, most of those who knew came from parents who had either dropped out of primary school or completed primary seven.

More than one half of the street children have parents who are mainly farmers or who work in marginal jobs in the informal sector. This finding is equally true for both sexes. Peasant farming and marginal jobs in the informal sector do not pay very well. With the increasing cost of living, these economic activities can barely help parents to get by. Most Tanzanians who engage in these activities live at a subsistence level and belong to what are considered the rural and urban poor. Marginal jobs, unemployment, and farming that does not go beyond subsistence lead to excessive poverty. Excessive poverty creates conditions that force parents to desert their children/families and children to run away in pursuit of greener pastures.

The simple fact that the incomes of these parents are not sufficient is also confirmed by street children's response to our question asking them to explain what they thought about their parent's income, whether it was enough, and why? Overall, 70% of the street children stated that it was not enough. About 289 children (71.1%) cited lack of food at home and failure of the parents to pay school-related expenses as

42

indicators that made them feel that their parent's income was not adequate. This kind of response is a clear indication of the fact that street children, regardless of age, are capable of evaluating a situation and understanding it. They are not always ignorant of the issues that directly touch and affect their lives.

In a way, this confirms our hypothesis that children are capable of scanning their social environment. Those who opt for life outside their families are more likely to engage in anything in order to survive, including illicit and criminal income-generating practices.

4.4 Street Children and Rural-Urban Migration

In any study of street children, knowing about the socio-economic characteristics of their parents and their family background does not necessarily provide us with comprehensive information about where they come from (rural or urban areas), patterns of their migration, or their reasons for leaving home. While associating family poverty with rural-urban migration is a valid, our study focused on listening to the voices of the street children themselves: where they came from, how they migrated to Dar-es-Salaam, and why.

Approximately 15% of the street children came from Coastal Region, 14% from Morogoro, 10% from Dodoma, 9% from Kilimanjaro, and 7% from Tanga. The majority stated that they originated from rural areas of these regions (80%). Why do these regions produce a greater number of Dar-es-Salaam's street children? There are a couple of reasons. The first is rural poverty. The rural areas of these regions are extremely underdeveloped and alternative sources of livelihood beyond farming are negligible. This does not mean that the situation is better in other regions, for the difference between these and other areas is only a matter of degrees. For example, compared to the Coastal, Morogoro, Tanga and Kilimanjaro regions, the rural part of Dodoma is the most underdeveloped area. In Kilimanjaro, social development has somehow penetrated even remote rural areas compared to the other regions. Land is very productive, but, due to population pressure, it is extremely scarce, and young people have difficulties getting easy access to the *"Kihamba"* (piece of land). What is unique to these regions as opposed to other regions is that they are very close to Dar-es-Salaam; Dar-es-Salaam is easily accessible by road, train or by foot for children coming from regions that boarder Dar-es-Salaam, such as Coastal, Morogoro, and Tanga. Looking at Table 2, above, it is evident that most regions with easy transportation to and direct communication with Dar-es-Salaam by road or train have a bigger share of street children living in Dar-es-Salaam as opposed to other regions. Hence, one can argue that, besides the comparative advantages that Dar-es-Salaam offers as a city, its nearness to the rural poor certainly makes it a target to the migrants. At the same time, we need to look at this process of young people drifting to cities within the context of processes of social change and development that are taking place in Tanzania at the moment. Rural electrification, which is taking place in some areas, particularly in sub-urban places, has exposed these places to the world of television and video. Marginalized youths and children regularly watch movies that glorify consumption habits that are beyond their and their parents' economic abilities. The new system of communication is bringing the life pattern of urban areas closer to the rural areas, and this raises the expectations of many people, particularly youths.

Most of the children mentioned poverty (58%), child abuse (10%), poverty and child abuse together (14%), and child abuse associated with step-parenting (61%), as the major reasons that forced them to leave their homes (Table 3). Step-parent abuse—as described by an orphaned girl of Ileje District, Tanzania below—can actually fuel the motive to migrate to urban areas in search of an alternative way of life.

"I am now twelve and live with my uncle. My mother died when I was seven. After five years, my father died too, and his brother then took me. My uncle and aunt have their own five children. One of their daughters is now 12 like me. I always do most of the domestic chores that includes cooking, laundry and fetching water. I am not allowed even to go to the church on Sundays. Their children attended confirmation classes and were recently confirmed. My aunt refused me to join them on grounds that someone had to be at home. I wish my parents were alive to see this happening." (Lugalla and Barongo 2000)

Table 2: Street Children's Reasons for Leaving Their Homes

S/N	REASON	NO. OF CHILDREN	PERCENTAGE
1	Poverty	234	58.1
2	Child Abuse	41	10.2
3	Both 1 & 2	58	14.4
4	Step-Parent Abuse	25	6.2
5	Both 2 & 3	10	2.5
6	Both 1 & 3	10	2.5
7	All of the above	7	1.7
8	Missing	18	4.5
	TOTAL	403	100.0

Source: Research Findings

Poverty is endemic in rural Tanzania; therefore, it is not surprising that children mention it as a major reason for migrating to cities. In terms of distribution, the recent Household Budget Survey revealed that 87% of the poor live in rural areas, as opposed to 13% in urban areas (HBS 2002). Poverty in a context of modernization and globalization has led to a situation whereby the authority of the older generation over important aspects of behavior, including sex, has been weakened. A young girl with access to wealthy men can bring home in an evening more than the official minimum monthly wage a normal worker receives. In view of this, some very poor parents are forced to use their children, particularly girls, in order to survive. Outwater (1996) has noted in Tanzania that parents fail to meet the basic needs of their children due to poverty. She has also noted how young girls enter into dangerous liaisons with older men, commonly known as "sugar daddies," so that, in exchange for sex, they can provide them with money to buy the latest fashions brought to Tanzania on the winds of modernization and globalization.

There was no significant difference between girls and boys in their reasons for leaving home. The only major difference was that for girls, step-parent abuse ranked third as opposed to fourth for boys. This difference suggests that harassment and probably sexual abuse might be common for girls living in step-parent households. A recent study of street children and orphans in Ileje district has noted the presence of extreme cases of abuse by step-parents (Lugalla and Barongo 2000). There is evidence from our findings that suggests that the street children's process of rural-urban migration is not a blind, haphazard one; rather, it is cumulative. Sixty-five percent of the children lived with relatives (43%) and friends (22%) when they arrived in Dar-es-Salaam for the first time. This is again confirmed by the fact that 49% stated they had been living in houses of friends or relatives in Dar-es-Salaam prior to resorting to street life. Only one third (34%) lived on street pavement immediately after their first arrival in the city. The analysis emerging from these findings is that most children do not simply leave their homes blindly. They scan the environment in their homes, contemplate where they want to go, and attempt to establish some kind of contacts in urban areas to assist them in getting used to the urban ways of life. Our in-depth interviews reveal that most children begin their journey to Dar-es-Salaam by spending a few months in nearby regional towns or cities. Very few indicated they had migrated to Dar-es-Salaam directly from rural areas. The response of one street girl below confirms the step-by-step migration process.

> "My cousin who lives in Dodoma town came and convinced me to accompany her to the town where she helped me in getting employed as a domestic servant. After working for three months, the wife of my uncle who lives in Dar-es-Salaam came and suggested to us that working, as a domestic servant in Dar-es-Salaam was more rewarding. So we left Dodoma, only to find that life in Dar-es-Salaam was difficult, jobs were hard to get. We finally ended up working as domestic servants, but then we left and started working on our own, getting money through our own means (prostitution)."

The belief that Dar-es-Salaam, as a big city, offers many opportunities to generate income, and that life is easier to manage seems to be very strong not only among street children, but also among many adults in Tanzania.

Dar-es-Salaam is a big city inhabited by very rich, affluent, middle class people and also by poor, very destitute people. It is the center of trade, industrial enterprises and political administration. Government offices, supermarkets, cinema theatres, bars, and restaurants are scattered throughout the city. As Diversi (1999) has observed for Campinas, Brazil, Dar-es-Salaam is crowded with people, some working, others shopping and others in transition. The Dalla-dalla buses complement the urban transport network system that makes almost every corner of Dar-es-Salaam reachable. The coexistence of wealth and poverty is conducive to employment opportunities, providing both marginal and formal white-collar jobs. This environment, with its rampant social inequality, creates an environment where begging, mugging, pick pocketing, and armed robbery can be cultivated and exercised. Children can make money by begging, vending, peddling, selling drugs, or stealing. Begging, eating leftovers from hotels, or surviving from garbage can easily become a source of food. The homeless can find accommodation in public toilets, schools, railway stations, discotheques or under parked cars. Dar-es-Salaam offers comparative advantages to rural homes, where life is completely a dead end with no other possibilities. For these reasons, not only Dar-es-Salaam, but also other large cities and urban centers in Tanzania become a target for the migrant poor—adults and children alike.

After learning the children's reasons for leaving their homes, we also wanted to know if they were willing to return home, and if not, why. Thirty percent were willing to go home because life in the city was cumbersome and very dangerous. Approximately two thirds (66.5%) were unwilling to go home, and cited the existence of poverty, no jobs, no parents and misunderstandings with the family as the major reasons causing them to be uninterested in going back to their homes. If street children are not interested in going back to their homes, then how do they survive in this seemingly harsh urban environment?

4.5 Children's Perceptions of Street Life and Coping Strategies

In order to understand the street children's experience of urban life and how they cope with it, we asked them a variety of questions requiring them to explain how they found food, accommodation, and other necessities of daily life. We began by wanting to know where they lived and with whom, and where they got their food.

Fifty-nine percent slept or spent their nights on street pavement and in unoccupied private and public buildings. Only 16% slept in railway and bus stations. There was no significant difference between boys and girls in terms of sleeping places (57.4% and 66.7% for boys and girls respectively). Only 9.4% lived in a children's home (Table 3).

Table 3: Where Street Children Live in Dar-es-Salaam

SN.	PLACE	NO. OF CHILDREN	PERCENTAGE
1	Street Pavement	118	29.3
2	Unoccupied Buildings	118	29.3
3	Railway/Bus Stations	65	16.1
4	Children's Home Buildings	38	9.4
5	Near Public Parks	12	3.0
6	Religious Buildings	8	2.0
7	Remand Houses	7	1.7
8	Other	31	7.7
9	No Response	6	1.5
	TOTAL	403	100.0

Source: Research Findings

Figure 5: Source of Income by Activities and Percentages

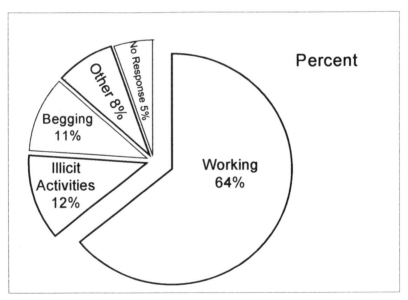

The majority (more than half) lived in groups comprised of their close friends who were also street children. Very few children lived alone. Street children form groups that function as a family. They walk and work in groups. Living in groups is one strategy that street children use in order to protect themselves from a dangerous outsider. Attacking one child means attacking the entire group. Social cohesion, solidarity, assistance, love and sympathy are found and felt within the group.

That life is not easy for these children is confirmed by what many of them indicated as the source of their daily meal. Approximately one half stated searching from the garbage as their main source of food, followed by hotel leftovers, begging and buying from shanty hotels (*magenge*). For those who buy food from shanty hotels, about two thirds earned their money working in the informal sector. Some worked as parking boys and others as car washers. Twelve percent cited illicit activities that included stealing, peddling drugs, prostitution or any other income generating activities that are not socially accepted in Tanzania. Twenty-three of the 51 girls cited illicit business (prostitution) as the source of their income. Eleven percent got their money by begging (Figure 5 and Table 4)

Table 4: Street Children's Sources in Income

SOURCE OF MONEY	NO. OF CHILDREN
Working	259
Illicit Activities	47
Begging	43
Other	32
No Response	22
TOTAL	403

Source: Research findings

49

For work, the children mentioned car parking, washing cars, petty trade, street vending, working as porters, and commercial sex. The average daily income from these activities varied along sexual lines. Most boys got not less than Tshs. 1000 ($1.50) but no more than Tshs. 2000 ($2.50) per day. Approximately one third of the girls (37.3%) earned below Tshs. 1000 per day, and 21% were like boys in their income. Only 13 girls got more than Tshs. 4000 per day. Operating as a prostitute varies a great deal in terms of income. Depending on operating zones and the nature of customers, some girls are likely to get a lot of money while others may end up with nothing except a beating for services they have provided. The response of the street girl below confirms this possibility.

> "Everyone has her own luck. Some sleep with tourists (particularly white men), and they end up paid not less than $10 per night (Tshs. 9000). Sometimes, if it is a bad day, you sleep with someone, and you end up being beaten and sexually abused without any pay at all. A friend of mine was seduced by a man who took her to an old unoccupied building where two men raped her. These men gave her nothing, but beat her up, robbed her watch, earrings, necklaces and clothes. She was left only with underwear. That is the situation. This business of ours is dangerous. But you have to do it in order to live in Dar-es-Salaam. You just keep on praying that you meet a nice guy." (Response from a Street Girl).

For boys, pick pocketing or general stealing, and, for girls, commercial sex, are not alien concepts at all. The need for money for food, clothes and other entertainment is a higher priority in the decision to commit a crime by robbing someone, or have paid survival sex with someone, than the hypothetical possibility that they can be caught, suffer from mob justice, become pregnant or get HIV or another sexually transmitted infection. As Diversi has observed with Brazilian street children, stealing a watch that will give them $5 in exchange, especially when their stomachs are growling or they are craving a drug that will temporarily free them from depressive consciousness of their condition, will likely outweigh the hypothetical notion of a cold cell in the event that they get caught (Diversi et al. 1999). These children live for the moment, as the narrative below suggests:

> "We have to survive in this environment. You do whatever is possible in order to get something for the day. We risk mob justice and being beaten to death. We spend a lot of time trying to dodge the police at the city offices. When we are caught, we are severely harassed. We always believe that being beaten by the mob or getting arrested is just like an

accident in the work place." (Response from a Street Boy, emphasis added)

One street girl responded to our female research assistant with the following:

"We exchange sex for money with anyone who can pay for the service, whether he is young or old, black or white, green or yellow, we don't care. *'Hapendwi mtu ila Pochi'* (We love the money but not the person). Most customers do not like condoms. So, we risk getting venereal diseases. I have contracted gonorrhea three times. Life is difficult, my dear sister. Be happy that your parents send you to school and that you are now a university student." (Response from a Street Girl).

These perceptions confirm that what is at stake is how to survive in a harsh urban environment and how to survive now/today. What makes the situation worse is the common belief held by the street children themselves, and even more so by other members of the society, that street children are useless, hopeless and dangerous young criminals who are likely to turn into hardcore criminals. Underlying this assumption is the conclusion that they have no future or chance in the mainstream social life in society. In one street child's own words,

"We are not living! We are dead already. Our bodies have no value in this society and everyone considers us worthless. Why should we value life that is basically not there? Our life is short, and therefore, we do whatever we can, legal or illegal –come what may." (Response from a Street Boy).

Although perceptions like these are dangerous and sometimes misleading, they are concrete in essence and are well-grounded based on the daily life and realities that these children experience. The attitudes, perceptions and behaviors that street children develop are not dropping from heaven like "*manna*" but are a product of social practice and experience in the harsh environment of Dar-es-Salaam. In order to combat these realities, street children pick-pocket, steal or practice survival sex, but they also drink alcohol and smoke cigarettes at a very tender age. While only 22% of the boys smoked ordinary cigarettes, about one half of the girls (41%) practiced this behavior. Although smoking cigarettes is less common for Tanzanian women and is highly stigmatized, it is increasingly becoming common among Westernized Tanzanian women and also prostitutes. Some smoke marijuana (*bhangi*), and take other dangerous drugs like cocaine, heroin and mandrax. One hundred and seventy street children (42%) knew some type of narcotics and had even used some of them. Children admitted to having used the following drugs (see Table 4.5 and Figure 6 below).

Table 5: Narcotic Drugs Ever Used by Street Children

N.	TYPE OF DRUG	NO. OF RESPONSES	PERCENTAGE
1	Marijuana	118	47.58
2	Mirungi	48	19.35
3	Cocaine	45	18.14
4	Heroine	23	9.27
5	Mandrax	14	5.64

Source: Research Findings

NB: Children were allowed to mention more than one drug ever used.

Figure 6: Narcotic Drugs Ever Used by Street Children

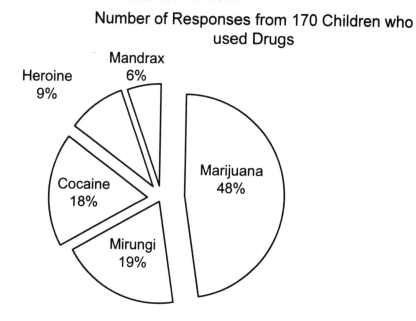

Number of Responses from 170 Children who used Drugs

Heroine 9%
Mandrax 6%
Cocaine 18%
Mirungi 19%
Marijuana 48%

Source: Computed from Table 4.5.

53

Our findings show that there is no significant difference between sexes in terms of the type of narcotics used. Bhang/marijuana seems to be equally popular among boys and girls. All children stated to have started using these narcotic drugs in Dar-es-Salaam. They had never heard about them in their rural areas. The children learn the names of these drugs and how to use them from their peers. Most children know that narcotic drugs are illegal and dangerous to their health. Nevertheless, they enter into these risky habits in order to cope with fear, hunger, and to make sure that their peers accept them. This is confirmed by a response of one street child:

"We are not stupid! We all know that these drugs are dangerous if you take more than enough. Even ordinary food can kill you if you take too much of it. We take drugs because they help us in dealing with these problems. With drugs at the top of your head, other humans look like ants. You feel strong and become a very carefree person." (Response from a Street Boy)

This response is supported by responses from other children to the question of why they used drugs. More than two thirds used drugs in order to cope with fear and difficulties, to get high, and to gain power and strength. They felt good after having taken them. There is a clear contradiction between street children's perception of drugs and how the society at large thinks about drugs. While for most people, and particularly law enforcement institutions, narcotic drugs are evil, dangerous, unfit for human consumption, and a health threat, they are part of the culture among youths in big cities in Tanzania. To the street children, drugs are a part of their solutions to the horrible life realities that they experience in urban areas. To them, using drugs is the best way of fighting fear, hunger and an unknown future in which they believe they only exist and do not live.

Street children are clever, imaginative and very tactical. In their pursuit for survival, they usually follow the rhythms of urban life. They ply the city center during business hours and retreat to their sleeping places at night. They are highly visible in congested trading business streets, near hotels, intersections, and particularly near traffic lights where the slow movement of the vehicles gives them an opportunity to either beg from drivers/passengers or to snatch someone's watch, earring, necklace or handbag. They usually ply railway and bus stations during departure and arrival times and attempt to earn an income either by working as porters, barkers (*Wapiga Debe*) or by stealing. The congestion of people in these areas tends to create a possible environment for street children to operate in legal and illegal activities. In the evenings and at night, most of them hover on the outside of restaurants, pubs, and in most cases, near dancing places and discotheques. The street vendors begin their work early in the morning and move from one street to the other. The parking boys, who also operate as car washers, locate themselves in specific open places where cars are allowed to park. They then direct car drivers to parking spaces and request to wash the cars and provide security in exchange for a few coins. Sometimes they wash the cars without even being told, with the hope that the owner will sympathize with them and give them something. Parking boys and prostitutes have divided the city into specific zones that they control. In-depth discussions of parking boys and girls reveal that the zoning system is theirs and that interference into other territories can result in serious conflicts with bitter consequences. In order to protect their zones and welfare, street children create peer relationships and networks of assistance among themselves. Street children have many friends of the same sex with whom they interact, walk and work. These friends provide company, often recruit new street children into groups and assist them in getting used to street life. Most of the street children of Dar-es-Salaam have lost their identity; therefore, their groups function as a surrogate family. Through a network of friends, street children learn not only new survival strategies, but also how to avoid the police and city officials.

4.6 Conclusion

This chapter has examined the nature of street children in Tanzania. Information derived from interviewing the street children themselves reveals that the majority of the children come from very poor, rural families. They have little or no formal education, and it is, therefore, very difficult for them to compete well in an open labor market in urban areas. There is concrete evidence emanating from this and other studies that most street children come from single parents or are orphans. Parents of street children work as subsistence farmers with hand-to-mouth, fluctuating incomes.

The findings presented in this chapter show that there are many factors generating street children. Besides rural and family poverty, other factors include lack of parents and/or maltreatment by relatives and child abuse at home and in school. In-school abuse often appears in the form of excessive physical punishments from teachers. Another factor is irrelevant education that trains children for white-collar jobs rather than providing solutions to local problems and needs.

Once in the urban streets, the children adopt different coping mechanisms. Some wash cars, beg, work as parking boys and practice commercial sex. Since street life is difficult, street children form and live in groups. Theses groups function as surrogate families. They assist children in identifying ways of survival by providing not only company, but also security and assistance to children in dodging the police or avoiding law enforcement institutions.

It is evident from our findings that children are not passive participants of processes aimed at improving their own welfare. Children evaluate their situations and the people who surround them. Some children know what they need in life in order to make their lives better, and others are capable of arranging priorities according to what they consider as important in life.

The analysis emerging from this is that it is important to listen to the voices of the children themselves if we want to assist them. Most of the street children we interviewed wanted support in education. Lugalla and Barongo noted a similar observation in their study of rural-based street and orphaned children in Ileje district. When children were asked to explain why they wanted to get an education or vocational training, most of them echoed the following response:

> *Elimu ni ufunguo wa maisha.*- Education is the key to life.-With education I can acquire a skill, get a good job and know a lot of things that can enable me to live a self-reliant life. (Lugalla and Barongo 2000)

Many street children we interviewed in Dar-es-Salaam also hold these views. Olenja and Kimani have recorded a similar observation in their study of child prostitution in Kisumu, Kenya. The fact that children's highest aspiration is education should be interpreted as a quest for productive skills that would facilitate access to basic needs. Therefore, any program for street children that pays attention to skill building will benefit the children a great deal. Such a program will not only rehabilitate them but also, as Olenja and Kimani have argued, will create independent, productive and responsible citizens.

Chapter 5

Children's Ethnographic Narratives of Urban Hardships and Violence

5.1 Introduction

"As children, we are always harassed and suffer much from both physical and verbal abuse. To whom can we report? It is the adults who treat us in this way. Even if you report to the police, these too do not trust what we say. The other thing is that if you report these problems to the police, you might risk being beaten again by the people you have reported"(Lugalla and Barongo, 2000).

Street children experience severe difficulties, hardships and violence everyday. They have difficulties in getting their basic daily needs and are always harassed and physically and verbally abused by both adults and law enforcement institutions. Since street children struggle for scarce resources in an urban environment, there is always cut-throat competition among children themselves and between children and street gangs of poor adults. Hence, conflicts are common: between children and adults, between children themselves, between employed children and their employers, and between street girls who are prostitutes and their customers and pimps. In this chapter, we present first some ethnographic accounts of street children's emic stories of the realities of urban life that reveal the nature of hardships and violence they experience. We have rewritten some stories in the form of conversation, dialogue, and events and actions so that readers can easily capture the difficulties of life. The narratives have been translated from colloquial Swahili to formal English. Although we have reconstructed some of these stories, we have tried our best to make sure that the voices of the children themselves are heard. We then associated these ethnographies with the empirical quantitative material on hardships and violence that the street children expressed in their survey questionnaire. To protect their identities, the children's names in these accounts have been changed.

5.2 Street Children and Urban Hardships

While the car of one of the co-authors (Joe Lugalla) was being washed in an open space near Avalon Cinema Hall in Dar-es-Salaam, Joe followed with keen interest the conversation of the two boys who were washing it. The conversation went as follows:

"You know, I have not been able to sleep for about four days now," said one boy.

"Why?" the other one replied.

The other boy continued to narrate the story as follows:

"On Monday, Juma and Ali, those friends of mine who wash cars near Mnazi Mmoja, came and told me that they knew one '*Mzungu wa Unga*' (a drug dealer) who had secured a '*mzigo*' ("luggage" meaning drugs) and wanted us to assist him in selling them to customers. They told me that he had promised to pay each of us 5000 shillings if we managed to sell within two days. Since the pay was attractive I accepted the deal. We went to the guy in Kariakoo and got the drugs. While there, the guy and his other two colleagues told us to deposit any amount of money and that we would get it back once we sold the drugs. They searched us, I had two thousand shillings, Juma had eight hundred, and Ali had one thousand seven hundred. They took all our money and said that was for security purposes in case we disappeared with their drugs. We then got the drugs and went to Manzese to look for that friend of ours, Mnoko."

"Who is he?" asked the one who was listening.

"You remember him. The one who was beaten almost to death by snatching an earring from a woman in a passing car on Ohio Street. And before that episode he sold crack to us in Mnazi Mmoja."

"Oh yes, now I remember him!" replied the listener and asked him, "So what happened?"

"I showed him the drugs and he said he knew a customer who would pay us good money. I gave him the drugs so that he would take them to the customer. We agreed that I should go there on the next day in the afternoon to get the money. I went to him on that day, but I did not find him. I have been looking for him now for almost three days, hunting him in his operating zones. But he is nowhere to be seen. That is why I told you I have not slept. I am afraid because Juma, Ali and the drug dealer are looking for me. Kimbutte met them yesterday and they asked him about me. He knows my whereabouts but he did not tell them where to find me because he noted that they were very furious."

"But why did you go to Mnoko. Don't you know that he is a swindler? You should have asked me. No one trusts him. He always swindles people just like that. Do you know Mapela?"

"Yes, I know him."

"He lost his five wrist watches because of Mnoko. Mapela got the watches from a domestic servant who works with an Asian shopkeeper. They must have stolen them. Mnoko promised to help Mapela sell the watches. He sold them and swindled the money, and threatened to report Mapela to the police. Many street children don't like him. He is evil. Don't trust him with anything. In fact, he can betray you and report you to the police."

"Yes you might be right." said the other one. "There was a time I saw him drinking Coca-Cola with a police officer. I wondered the kind of relationship they had. In fact, the day when he was beaten almost to death it was members of his own group who betrayed him, by identifying him as the person who had snatched the earring. I think they wanted to teach him a lesson. Now give me some advice, what should I do in order to get either money or my drugs back?" asked the first boy.

"Forget about Mnoko! You are going to get nothing from him!" replied the other and continued to say, "The best thing is to collect the money and pay the drug dealer. Otherwise he will also beat you to death. How much is the money for the drug dealer?"

"15,000 Tshs."

"Let us work together to pay that money. '*Tusaidiane sisi ni marafiki leo ni wewe, kesho ni mimi*' (Let's help each other, we are friends. Today you are in trouble, tomorrow I will be in trouble.)"(Lugalla Field Notes March 7,2000).

One of our research assistants recorded the following conversation during the fieldwork in Ilala District;

"Do you know what happened yesterday in Manzese?" Poka asked his friend Joka.

"No! What happened?" replied Joka.

"There were so many police officers and militias there yesterday. They have been looking for two boys who stole a bag from a tourist in Mnazi Mmoja."

"Now why did they go to Manzese?" asked Joka.

"I do not know why, but I understand that someone told the police that those two suspects were street boys who usually operate and sleep in Manzese."

"Now did they find them there?" asked Joka.

"No, I am not sure. But I am told the police visited all the places street children frequent most including their sleeping places. They arrested more than twenty children and detained them. The children who were arrested were beaten and harassed, and I understand some of them have been detained at either Magomeni or Central Police Station."

"Are the police still there?" asked Joka.

"I am not sure. But for today, Manzese is not a nice place for us to go. You know they can arrest you even if they just see you walking in the street. You know Joka," said Poka, "Street children have no rights. We are nothing in front of the police and in front of the people in general. When the police beat you up, no one helps. When the ordinary people harass or beat you, the police don't rescue you. Do you remember that last year in Mburahati, Masumbuko was beaten to death by the mob for suspecting him of stealing a mobile phone? You and I were there, when one angry person smashed the head of Masumbuko with a heavy cement block and ended his life?"

"We need to be very careful nowadays." Joka responded. "The people have their own problems, and we are always the ones responsible for their problems. So if they arrest you stealing or even if they simply suspect you they finish you immediately."

"You are right Joka." Poka responded. "In fact, my friend Jengo and I were planning to go to Manzese and Mabibo today to accomplish a certain 'misheni'" (dubious deal or plan.) "But because of the police patrol in Manzese, I am scared."

"What was the deal about?"

"Ask me later, I will tell you."(Research Assistant, Field Notes June 13, 1999)

On April 28, 2000 one of our researchers recorded the following statement from a street boy:

"Many people, including you, look at us negatively and are always suspicious. Most people believe that we are dangerous, we steal, we take drugs, and we should be removed from the city like what the Regional Commissioner of Dar-es-Salaam, Mr. Yusufu Makamba did recently with beggars. Let me tell you, my dear brother. You see that friend of mine washing that car over there? He and I have been doing this job since we arrived in Dar-es-Salaam from Morogoro five years ago. Stealing and robbing someone are foreign concepts to us. We survive in this city by showing car drivers where to park. We wash the cars and provide security. The minimum we get for each car is Tshs. 200 if we just provide security. If we clean it we get not less than Tshs. 500 per day. Everyday my friend and I have more than ten customers. Why then should I be involved in dangerous and risky activities of stealing? We use clean methods to get our daily food. But the police keep on harassing us. City officers argue that we are not registered car washers, we do not pay tax, and we are young criminals. In order to avoid all this, we sometimes share with the police and city fathers what we get. We bribe them so that they can turn their eyes the other way. It is poverty, which is forcing us to survive in this way. Both of us lost our parents.

We are told it was AIDS that killed them."(Research Assistant, Field Notes April 28, 2000)

A young street girl aged 15 explained her ordeal to our female research assistant as follows:

"I came to Dar-es-Salaam when I was twelve. I had already dropped out of school in the fifth grade because my uncle who was taking care of me after the death of both my parents could not manage to pay the school expenses. My aunt brought me to Dar-es-Salaam and sent me to her woman friend, who had a big family, husband and four children, where I began working as a domestic servant for a wage of Tshs. 3000 per month. I had to cook, clean the house, wash the dishes, do the laundry, go shopping, and take care of the garden and their poultry unit with 200 chickens. I smelled like chicken everyday, and the woman would complain that I was dirty and smelling, and therefore I was not allowed to eat with them. I was always told to eat leftovers in the kitchen and not with them at the dining room table. But I did not mind all this. What made me quit is the wage. I was not being paid. The woman told me that she was paying my aunt, who in turn told me that she was keeping the money for me. Finally, a friend of mine (another domestic servant from a nearby house) introduced me to her sister, who worked as a barmaid in Keko-Machungwa area. She convinced both of us to leave our employers, which we did, and she assisted us in getting new jobs as barmaids. I became so happy because smelling chicken dung would now be a thing of the past. However, new problems arose. The bar owner paid us according to the number of bottles we sold. In order to sell many bottles of beer, one must attract many customers as their waitress. This means that one must be charming, attractive and sometimes must respond positively to their sexual advances. At the beginning, I got very few customers because I was always reluctant to accept their sexual advances. But other girls (barmaids) told me that it was our own fault. They advised us that if we wanted to succeed as barmaids in Dar-es-Salaam we had no option. We had to accept sexual advances from our customers. The first time I decided to try, my customer gave me Tshs. 10,000 for spending a night with him in a guesthouse. He bought beer for himself and me, and he also paid for a barbecued chicken that we ate together. From there on, my friend and I began practicing survival sex. Finally, we decided to quit working as barmaids after realizing that we could still get money by visiting beer pubs and interacting with male customers. We wanted to enjoy our freedom. We learned this from other girls who had always been visiting our bar as customers and ended up getting male partners every day. So, we decided to assert our independence by being free-lance prostitutes."

When our researcher asked this girl if she was comfortable with her current profession, her response was:

"Yes and No. We now get a lot of money. So, getting food, clothing, and perfumes is no longer a big problem. The problem is that you operate with a lot of uncertainties. Most customers do not want to use condoms. So, getting venereal diseases is the order of the day. I have contracted sexually transmitted diseases five times now. I became pregnant twice, and through the help of other girls, I got treatment and abortions. But, I am always scared that I might end up dying of HIV/AIDS. Anyway, "God knows and Helps". I have to survive in Dar-es-Salaam. The other uncertainty is with the police. They call us 'Changu Doa' (urban street prostitutes). Everyone labels us with that name. The people yell at us, and sometimes we are arrested by the police and detained. I have been arrested three times, and I spent one night at Oyster Bay police station and two nights at Keko Remand Prison. We usually bribe in order to get our freedom. I know of some girls who have been arrested then accused of loitering and finally sentenced to 6 months in prison. The Swahili people normally say 'Ng'ombe wa maskini hazai, akizaa, huzaa dume' (The cow of poor person never gives birth, if it does, it usually delivers a male calf)."

5.3 Street Children and Violence

NICHO'S STORY

Nicho is now 15 years old. He dropped out of school when he was in the fifth grade because his uncle could not afford to pay for school fees. Both of his parents died when he was 5 years old. The following is a brief story of how he ended up coming to Dar-es-Salaam. Following Nicho's narrative are similar stories told by other boys who have taken to the streets.

"My aunt always accused me of being a thief. She and my uncle used to beat me almost every day. One day, she realized that the oxen plowing blade was missing. She accused me of stealing it and selling it to other farmers. She locked me up in a dark room for the whole day without food, waiting to report to my uncle when he came back. I really knew that I would be in severe trouble when he came back. So I decided to escape. I waited until it was dark and escaped through the window without the notice of my aunt. I went to Makambako, boarded the train up to Dar-es-Salaam. I spent the first three nights at the railway station eating from garbage. Then the next day, a police officer arrested me. I was locked in the police cell at Buguruni for one day. Finally, a good Samaritan took me to the ferry area where she introduced me to other street children who in turn taught me how to survive by scraping fish shells. It is these children who showed me the Dogo Dogo Center for Street Children, where I lived for a while. We used to get food and accommodation at the center, but not money. Since I was interested in making my own money, I left the center and went back to the ferry area to continue with the working of scraping fish. I normally get no less than Tshs. 500 a day. But, then sometimes the adult street gangs harass and beat us, and require money from us in exchange for protection. Sometimes at night they also want to have anal sex with us. I usually refuse, and instead give them money whenever they ask for such a game. So life is not easy. But I would rather stay here and earn my own money instead of going back to my home area and be treated like an animal. It is difficult to live here, but at least I have my freedom and can make my own money."

NESCO

"I am 15 years old. My mother and father died when I was 7 and 9 years old respectively. So I moved from our home and started living with my elder brother. He could not afford to pay the school fees, so I dropped out of school and started working on the farm from Monday to Sunday. Sometimes he would deny me food, and would beat me up if I woke up late or did something wrong on the farm. One day a friend of mine suggested that we travel to Dar-es-Salaam to look for work. He told me that in Dar-es-Salaam life would be easier. After all, there were many organizations that assisted orphans, so we were likely to improve our welfare by migrating there. So we left. When we arrived in Dar-es-Salaam, we spent our nights at Mnazi Mmoja bus station, washing and guarding the parked buses. We slept in the buses for almost two months. One night, the police invaded us, beat us up, and took our belongings, including our money. They took us to Central Police Station, where we were detained for three days. Then we were taken to the remand prison in Keko where we stayed for about a month. Life in the remand prison was terrible and horrible. We ate only once a day. We were put together with adult inmates. Some of my colleagues were sexually molested. Look at all this skin disease I acquired when I was there, and have not managed to get treatment up to now because I have no money."

TUMBO

"I am fifteen years old. I come from a poor family in Tabora Region. My mother died soon after my birth and my father died six years later. After the death of my mother, my sister took me. Although she was poor, she was able to send me to school because she had a child of the same age who was going to school. But life in school was horrible. The teachers punished us daily for not having books and writing materials like notebooks and pencils. Two other children and I decided to run away from our home village and came to Dar-es-Salaam in 1998. We left home at midnight and walked on foot for three days before boarding a train. Lack of adequate food supplies at home, child abuse at school and lack of parental love are factors that made us leave our homes. When we arrived in Dar-es-Salaam, we were advised to go to Dogo Dogo Center for street children. We lived there for a certain period, and then left because we wanted to make our own money in the streets. Life in the street is also difficult. There is no reliable source of food, police are harassing us, and fellow street children are a threat to us too. One day, I was confronted by a group of street children and they cut my leg with a sharp object. Insecurity and violence have dominated urban life. Once you are in confrontation with either other street children or police, there is no one to help you. Diseases are also a problem because I have no money to pay for treatment and also no money for food and other demands. Once I fall sick, I have to seek assistance from various people. There are some friends who provide me with help, but sometimes they ignore me. When such a situation happens, life becomes more difficult. I have to walk for almost the whole day trying to get just a few coins for food. I do not use drugs or alcohol. I am afraid to use them because I am always searching for employment. If people find me drunk and realize that I smell of alcohol they will never take me. In spite of these difficulties, I have no desire to go back home because I have nothing left there. There is no home, there are no parents, so there is no need of going there. First of all, no one needs me there. Although I am tired of street life, I would rather live here than go back home."

The ordeal of Masalakulangwa, below, also reveals the nature of violence experienced at home and in the streets.

"I am a 16-year-old boy from Singida. I came to Dar-es-Salaam two years ago. I decided to engage in street life as a solution to the problems I was facing back home. Both of my parents died some time ago. However, my problems started before their deaths. I am from a poor family, but my parents did not love me at all. This is because they were bewitched. I remember one day, I stole a piece of meat from the cooking pot, and my mother burned my hand until I fainted. After the death of my parents, relatives took me in to live with them, but there the situation was even worse. There were uncertainties in getting food. Whenever I went to play outside and came back, they always told me that the food was finished, so I had to sleep without eating. One day when I asked why there was no food for me, I was told it's because I do not belong to that family. Sometimes, I was forced to work in the neighbor's fields so I could get food. Hard work and severe punishments were the order of the day. I was supposed to feed animals every day, which was very difficult work for me, and when I refused, there was a severe punishment. These punishments were intolerable, as they were too severe. One day, my uncle cut me with a razor blade on the back because I didn't take the animals grazing. Another day, I was beaten until I lost consciousness. These were the driving forces that made me shift from Singida to Dar-es-Salaam. When I first arrived in Dar-es-Salaam, I used to live on the street pavements. Later, I shifted to Dogo Dogo Center where I was registered as a street child and began a new life. Together with other children, I started training as a musician. Although I was treated fairly at Dogo Dogo, I was still in touch with my friends outside Dogo Dogo. They taught me to smoke, to use drugs and drink alcohol. These drugs were and are still good to me, as they help me to forget all the difficulties I face. I drink *gongo* (illicit brew), and I use marijuana, beer and cigarettes. These things give me power to confront the police without fear. Because of using drugs and alcohol, I was kicked out of the Dogo Dogo Center. Now I am completely living in streets where there is no security, but a lot of harassment. Police are beating us; street gangs beat us and take the money we get away from us. Getting food is a problem. I am living by begging, car washing and doing other illicit activities. But all these activities cannot provide enough money to enable me to meet my demands. When I am sick, it is also a problem. There are some friends who help either to pay for my treatment or sometimes buy me some drugs, but they sometimes refuse. If someone wants to pay for my education, I am ready to change and I will stop using drugs and alcohol. Going to school may help me to change my life and I may be able to get out of all these problems."

Although sexual harassment and abuse seem to be exercised on both boys and girls, there is evidence from individual street children, focus groups, urban residents and law enforcement institutions that street girls and women in general tend to be the most victimized. Below are some testimonies from street girls on the nature and type of violence they experience in urban settings.

"Everyone believes that we are bad and that we embarrass women. I believe you too think the same way." Responded a street girl to our female research assistant.

"Why do you think so?" the researcher asked the girl.

"You know my dear sister, you call us *'Changu-Doa,'* *'Malaya'* (prostitutes) *'fuska'* (promiscuous people), and *'Wanawake wachafu'* (dirty women). These names are familiar to everyone living in Dar-es-Salaam. From these names, you can understand that everyone does not like us. But the truth of the matter is that we are individuals who are free to do whatever we want. We patrol the streets at night in pursuit of our fortune—Life! Survival! We have no work. We neither disturb people who are sleeping nor do we follow people in their homes. It is the men themselves who leave their houses to come to us. They give us money in exchange for sex. The women who blame us are stupid! They should deal with their husbands and not us. All men who talk bad things about us are hypocrites. They curse us during the day, but embrace and pay us at night. The police harass us every day, but sometimes they demand sex in exchange of our freedom. You think we are interested in sleeping with several men whom we do not know everyday? It is a risky job. Sometimes they rape us. They beat us, they rob us, or they refuse paying us for services that we have provided them. Think of all this!! Life is not easy." (Street girl aged 16 years).

∞

Another street girl explained her experience of street life as follows:

"One evening, an adult guy invited me to barbecued meat and beer in a shanty restaurant in Vingunguti. He wanted me to accompany him to his house. I agreed. I knew he wanted to have sex with me. I accepted, because I knew if I refused, I would have invited serious trouble. While at his slum house, he raped me several times. He then forced me to have sex with his two roommates. They finally hired a taxi and dumped me in Magomeni area around midnight. I could not report them to the police, since I knew the police would not help me. Besides that, I did not know the people and could not remember the house since I was drunk that night. After a few days, I missed my monthly periods and finally realized that I was pregnant. When I went to the hospital, the doctor said I had syphilis and gonorrhea, too. I delivered safely and got treatment for the venereal diseases. My daughter is now living in an orphanage." (Street girl aged 15)

∞

"One day at midnight, near Oyster Bay Hotel, a group of five adult boys (a street gang) surrounded a friend of mine and I. They grabbed us, took us to the beach and stripped us naked. While there, they forced us to smoke marijuana and drink beer while raping us in turns. These problems are common to us. Every street girl has experienced them at least once. Some of us have now decided to befriend street gangs of adult boys. They protect us and sometimes hook us up with male customers. We usually offer them both money and sex for this service. If

68

you refuse to pay them in this way, the consequences can be severe or even fatal. Usually when you read in newspapers that a dead body of a woman has been found lying somewhere, most of these deaths are a result of this. I have no doubt that I will certainly die of HIV/AIDS. If you tell them to use condoms, they do not listen. If you stop performing survival sex, you die anyway, due to lack of food. So what is the alternative? (Street girl aged 14 years)

∞

"I am now 17 years old. I came to Dar-es-Salaam from Singida Region when I was 11 years old. I then worked as a domestic servant for one year. I quit the job and worked as a barmaid for two years. I began working as a street commercial sex worker when I was 15. Within the last two years, I have been raped four times, suffered from gang rape twice, have aborted three times and have contracted sexually transmitted diseases several times." (Street girl aged 17 years)

∞

"I came to Dar-es-Salaam three years ago. I was 14 and had just completed my primary education. A woman from our home village in Tabora is the one who brought me to Dar-es-Salaam and wanted me to assist her in her business. I assisted her in selling local brew (*Komoni*, *Kimpumu* and *Mbege*). She provided me with accommodation and food. After a few months, she started telling me to spend some nights with some men. When I refused, she became angry, and insulted me terribly, she said that I was an idiot, I had to wake up, and that this was the way of life, if I wanted to survive in Dar-es-Salaam. One night, I had sex with one customer. He was so rough and demanded both vaginal and anal sex. When I refused to comply with the demand of anal sex, he beat me up, yelled at me, and said he had paid the woman already. So what he needed from me was service, otherwise he would kill me. This woman continued to exploit me for almost a year, until some of my friends convinced me to leave. They told me that I would make more money if I sold sex independently rather than being under this woman." (Street girl aged 17 years)

What the above narratives reveal is the exploitation of these young girls by adults. In-depth discussions in focus groups revealed that sexual exploitation of street girls is rampant in Dar-es-Salaam. The exploitation operates at different levels. First, street girls are molested sexually; they experience traumatic and rough sex and sometimes end up not being paid for the services they have provided. Secondly, the pimps and bouncers who provide them with security and connect them with customers demand sex and money as the medium of exchange for their services. Thirdly, some adult women accommodate some young girls in their brothels, link these girls to male customers and instruct the men to pay them instead of paying the girls who physically provide the service. Our focus groups also revealed that, at present, there are women in Dar-es-Salaam who recruit domestic servants from upcountry areas. These women usually instruct the employers to pay them the salaries of domestic workers instead of paying the domestic servants themselves.

5.4 Narratives and Stories as Life Experiences

The brief narratives of street boys and girls describing their daily experience of what the urban environment offers reveal a variety of issues. It is evident that street children need a lot of intelligence, energy and attention in order to survive successfully in a harsh urban environment. As we were writing this report, *The Guardian* newspaper of Tanzania had the following information on its front page:

"About 30 street children have invaded the center for vocational education and a hostel for street children located at Ipogolo in the Iringa town even before it starts operating. According to one of the children, they invaded the center on March 9, 2001 after failing to cope with difficulties they were experiencing in the streets. "Sleeping in ditches, running away from police brutalities are some of the problems we were experiencing." (*The Guardian*, March 29, 2001)

As has been observed elsewhere, the children must struggle to get food every time they are hungry, must be very imaginative just to bathe, must find a different place to sleep every night, and must stay away from angry drug dealers and police while confined to public spaces (Diversi 1999). In Kenya, street girls, unlike street boys, are much more vulnerable to physical attack and report being raped by street boys (Kilbride *et al.* 2001). We noted a similar observation in Tanzania. There is concrete evidence that life in urban streets is organized in a hierarchical manner with older boys exercising authority and power over younger ones and street girls, too.

70

For most street girls, practicing survival sex is a strategy to obtain shelter, food and security. It is not a wonder that what may appear as exploitation in our eyes is a blessing from their perspective (Olenja and Kimani 2000). Some of the hazards in this occupation include fighting for clients with fellow prostitutes and beatings from clients, especially when one does not live up to the bargain (ibid). In Tanzania, loitering and prostitution are both illegal; therefore, being harassed by the police is common to both street boys and girls. Street children are severely discriminated against in the urban system. They are always considered guilty before they are even sent to the court. In most cases, they cannot defend themselves, and sometimes they end up locked in detention centers for crimes they have not committed. In reality, there is no equality between street children and other members of the mainstream society before the law. Similar to what Shorter and Onyancha (1999) have observed in Nairobi, most of the street children we interviewed revealed that they had been assaulted in some ways, slapped, kicked, physically or sexually abused and even risked being lynched (ibid).

The narratives and stories above reveal the nature of police brutality against street children. Street children who have ever been arrested by the police describe their experience under police custody as horrendous. They describe being put in the same cells with adults where forced anal sex buys one security and protection from further maltreatment by adult inmates. They cite cases of being denied food for days or given delayed and smelling cornmeal served with half-cooked beans. They narrate sleeping on the floor without blankets or sleeping garments. Some of them recall the ordeal of sleeping in their own urine and filth for days and state that by the time they came out of jail, they had contracted a variety of infectious diseases. If we compare these narratives and stories with empirical findings, we learn that what was echoed in individual narratives is basically experienced by almost all street children. A total of 354 children out of 403 (88%) confirmed that life in Dar-es-Salaam was not easy. They also argued that they experienced severe hardships and horrible forms of violence in their daily lives. As Table 5.1 below shows, more than half stated that they experienced most of the problems listed in the table below.

71

Table 6: Types of Hardship Experienced by Street Children

SN	TYPE OF HARDSHIP	NO. OF CHILDREN	PERCENTAGE
1	Life is not safe	61	15.1
2	Food insecurity	22	5.5
3	Molestation/Being Beaten by Adults	25	6.2
4	Harassment by Law Enforcement	43	10.7
5	Most of the Above	330	7
6	Missing	19	4.7
	TOTAL	403	100.0

Source: Research Findings

Three quarters of the children (74.7%) indicated that being beaten and harassed was the order of the day. They mentioned street gangs, city officials and law enforcement institutions as notorious sources of harassment and beatings. As enemies, most of the street children mentioned street gangs (42%) and the police (41%). As friends, 68% mentioned their fellow street children. Only two children out of 403 mentioned the police as friends, 7% cited street gangs and 9.9% considered street children centers as friendly. There was no significant difference in these responses between boys and girls. The analysis emanating from these findings is that street children are also suspicious of street children centers. Many join them but end up opting out after a while. The experience of these children is full of abuse and violence exercised by people close to them, and this makes them mistrustful and fearful of society's institutions. They do not believe that institutions are there to help them. The trends Diversi observed in Brazil are also true of street children in Dar-es-Salaam. Their only guiding hope seems to lie in the immediate and concrete rewards of the streets: acceptance among peers (also engaged in activities perceived as "deviant" by society), drug "trips" and the freedom of an unsupervised life (Diversi 1999). By developing specific strategies or skills of coping with urban life, street children easily win recognition from other street children who always end up acknowledging or accepting such strategies. However, as Smollar (1999) has argued for the homeless youth of the United States, because those skills of surviving often include shoplifting, stealing, swindling, pick-pocketing, prostitution, and begging, they are not consistent with skills valued by mainstream society. Hence, the kind of competency those children acquire as a result of coping with street life usually hinders them from becoming integrated into the mainstream social life of the Tanzanian society (ibid). The adaptive strategies children invent help them to connect to each other, but fail them in making sure that they re-connect with their families and society at large (ibid). In fact, studies elsewhere have shown that the most difficult youth to reach with services are often those who have achieved the greatest success in adapting to street life (Luna 1987, Smollar *et al.* 1986). A brief discussion with social workers of some Tanzanian street children NGOs reveals that the above observation is equally true for Tanzania. The terms often used to describe such children, *"Sugu"* ("hard core") or *"Magangwe"* ("care free") in the Swahili language, imply that "chronic street children" are difficult to retain in rehabilitation programs offered by various NGOs.

The fact that these children are skeptical of adults and law enforcement institutions is evidenced by their response to questions about where they seek protection or assistance when they were in difficulties or serious trouble. One quarter (25%) sought assistance from their fellow street children, 10% and 6% from social and legal institutions respectively. The children stated that they received moral, emotional and material support from their peers when they were in difficulties and that their peers provided them with security, too. More than two thirds lived in groups and used a variety of methods of self-defense in order to protect themselves. Living in the streets without parental supervision places children at greater risk of deviant behaviors. It produces an environment conducive to children associating themselves with health risks and antisocial behavior like taking drugs and alcohol at an early age, sexual activity, robbery and violence, and other behaviors that put them again at risk with both the police and the civil society.

5.5 Conclusion

In this chapter we have presented a variety of narratives and stories from the street children. The narratives and stories represent the voices of the marginalized children themselves, what they experience, the hardships and violence they endure, how they evaluate themselves and perceive the people and institutions that surround them.

While it is clear from this ethnographic information that both street boys and girls experience a variety of hardships and violence, sexual violence like gang rape, sexual abuse and harassment tend to characterize most the lives of street girls. These problems, as statistics will reveal in the next chapter, explain why some street girls tend to suffer from sexually transmitted diseases more than street boys. Since prostitution is illegal and is considered as immoral by the mainstream society, street girls who practice survival sex are shunned and harassed by street boys, street gangs, the police and ordinary adult citizens. These gender differences between street boys and girls suggest a need to rethink the way in which street children are perceived by the members of the mainstream society as well as by law enforcement institutions. The hardship and violence discussed in this chapter lay the foundation for us to understand the impact of street life on street children's health, which is the subject matter of the following chapter.

Chapter 6

Street Life and Street Children's Health

6.1 Introduction

Having seen how street children cope with urban life, the hardships and violence they experience, and how they deal with these problems, it is also important to understand how street life impacts children's health. This is the subject matter of this chapter. We have divided the chapter into four main sections. The first is the introduction. The second section is a general discussion on how street life and social environment makes children vulnerable to ill health. The third section presents the survey findings, which reveal the types of diseases that children mentioned as disturbing them most. We also present some stories that reflect street children's experience with health issues. In the fourth section, we attempt to collaborate our findings for health issues with concrete data collected from the Dar-es-Salaam Youth Health Clinic.

6.2 Street Life and Health

It is evident from the findings of our study that street life is difficult, and when exacerbated by deplorable urban conditions, the health of street children comes under serious threat. Street children are always exposed to hazardous and very horrifying cultural practices that endanger their well being as well as developmental abilities. In order to cope with life, some take drugs, practice survival sex and engage in other underground activities on a daily basis that not only affect them physically, but emotionally and psychologically.

For example, in their attempts to avoid hunger, fear, and the dire need to be accepted by friends or peers, street children frequently take drugs; thus, drug taking tends to be a much higher priority for them than the abstract threats of negative health consequences preached by health education advocates. Fighting for immediate needs seems more realistic to most street children and may influence their decisions to have unprotected sexual encounters more so than the hypothetical fear of becoming pregnant and/or contracting a severe or even deadly venereal disease like HIV/AIDS. Young people, not only in Tanzania but in sub-Saharan Africa, are increasingly faced with decisions regarding risky behavior. They are confronted with easy access to addictive substances and lethal weapons and the potentially lethal consequences of unprotected sexual activity. Both of these behavior tendencies are influenced by the

75

economic and cultural pressures faced by young people, who are often forced to drop out of school for a variety of reasons, in the face of competitive job markets requiring higher education to be able to earn a decent salary (Kaaya *et al.* 1997).

As Diversi (1999) has argued for street children of Campinas, Brazil, identity formation is one of the developmental problems that these street children experience. Street children's sense of self is experienced in a particularly unfriendly social context (Diversi 1999). Identity, especially at the beginning stages of adolescence, is largely shaped by the ways in which others view and interact with an individual, and is thus dependent on a dialogical relationship between the individual and his or her social environment (Mead 1934, Diversi 1999). If this is true, one can certainly see how street children in Dar-es-Salaam suffer as far as processes of identity formation are concerned. Most people look at street children with suspicion. They treat them as "young criminals" who have to be dealt with while they are still young. Most people believe, "*Samaki Mkunje Angali Mbichi, akikauka atavunjika*" (Bend the fish while fresh, otherwise it will break). The police and city officials often treat them as guilty criminals even in situations where they have done nothing wrong. Everything they do is associated with deviant behavior and very unlikely to be approved of by the mainstream society. These are the day-to-day experiences of these children, and hence, the children themselves end up evaluating themselves along the same lines. They usually regard themselves as useless, dead and condemned by the entire society. The impact of these experiences in terms of the psychosocial well being of these children is always negative. Most street children are psychologically traumatized, having been robbed of the experience of childhood and having been forced to adopt adult roles at a tender age (Shorter and Onyancha 1999). As Shorter and Onyancha have observed in street children of Nairobi, Kenya, all these factors inhibit the intellectual, emotional and physical growth of street children. They argue that street children are physically small for their age, since chronic malnutrition has stunted their physical growth (Shorter and Onyancha 1999).

The majority of street children have no proper living or sleeping places that conform to normal minimum and basic health standards. Most of them live simply on street pavement, in old, dilapidated, unoccupied buildings or buildings that are under construction. Some hover on the periphery of railway and bus stations, discotheques and religious buildings. They usually fight not only for food, but also for sleeping places and clothing. They usually lack sufficient clothing, and can dress in one set of clothes for months without washing them. Their bed clothing is often no more than newspapers or cardboard (Shorter and Onyancha 1999). Street children do not have permanent sleeping places. In fact, having different sleeping places is also a coping strategy of evading the police and city fathers. Even if they find a permanent sleeping

76

place, they are usually chased away by watchmen and other security guards who patrol the city at night. Sometimes, they have to secure a good sleeping place by bribing the guards with money or sex. In general, street children live in an urban environment that manufactures epidemics and diseases. Facilities for health and sanitation are lacking, and street children have severe difficulties maintaining their personal hygiene.

Street children have severe difficulties accessing clean places to bathe. More than a quarter (26%) bathe in public water kiosks. Fifteen percent use rivers, most of which are contaminated with human and chemical wastes (Kondoro et al. 1996). Nine percent and 8% used natural ponds and seawater respectively, and about 10% illegally use the showers available at the railway and bus stations. As sources of their drinking water, the street children cite shanty hotels (51%), rivers and public water kiosks (22%), railway stations and natural ponds (4% and 5% respectively). Table 7 below reveals how street children dispose of their human waste. It is evident from this data that places where the children dispose of their human waste are unreliable. Although approximately 26% mentioned public toilet facilities, the reality is that most public toilets in Dar-es-Salaam are no longer operational. Nowadays, those that function have introduced user fees and cannot be used without paying. Most street children would rather keep their savings for food. Using toilet facilities at the bus/railway stations is also problematic. For example, in order to enter the Ubungo main bus terminal in Dar-es-Salaam, one needs to show either a bus ticket indicating that he/she is traveling or has to buy an entrance ticket. This hinders many street children from using toilet facilities that are in the bus terminal. Even if one has an entrance ticket, one is still required to pay a user fee in order to use the toilet facilities at the bus terminal. We also noted during our study that toilet facilities at the Central Railway Line Station and the Tanzania/Zambia Authority Station are also beyond the reach of the street children. There are security guards who usually monitor people who enter the premises of these respective railway stations. In view of this, hidden bushes and other inappropriate places remain the only places possible.

Table 7: Where Street Children Dispose Their Human Waste

S/N	TOILET FACILITY	NO. OF CHILDREN	PERCENTAGE
1	Public Toilet	103	25.6
2	Hidden Streets	65	16.1
3	Railway/Bus Station	60	14.9
4	Nearby Bushes	29	7.2
5	Sea Side	22	5.5
6	Public Parks	2	0.5
7	Other	89	22.1
8	No Response	35	8.1
	TOTAL	403	100.0

Source: Research Findings

6.3 Street Children's Common Diseases

There is no doubt that the unhealthy urban environment in which these children live is a major cause of health problems among them. A recent study of street children in Tanzania noted that all children mentioned malaria, diarrhea, stomach-related illnesses, coughing and other respiratory diseases like pneumonia, asthma and others as diseases that affected them most (Lugalla and Mbwambo 1999). These findings revealed that infectious diseases were common among street children. There is no doubt that this is a result of a variety of predisposing factors which include unsafe and unhygienic sleeping areas, the shortage or lack of safe drinking water, unsafe food, leftovers and food collected from garbage bins (ibid.). A study in Nairobi, Kenya found that on average, a street child was more likely to die of diseases commonly afflicting children than a school-going child, because prevention is impossible on the street, and in most cases, immunization campaigns often target school children and/or infants in post-natal care, but do not address other categories of children (Shorter and Onyancha 1999). The street children of Tanzania experience the same fate. Even if medical services were available to street children, there is no parental supervision to ensure compliance (ibid.). In a situation where most health care facilities charge user fees, street children are more likely to refrain from using health services because they cannot afford them. In Dar-es-Salaam, there is a youth health clinic owned by the City Council that offers free medical and immunization services. Ignorance and lack of access to appropriate information about health create a situation whereby street children are less likely to seek free vaccinations and health care services than a child who is attached to a well-functioning, responsible family. All these factors contribute simultaneously to put many children in a very vulnerable situation of ill health.

In order to understand the magnitude of health problems experienced by street children, we asked them to mention more than one disease. Most responses indicated malaria (68%), diarrhea (30%), related skin diseases (51%), Bilharzia (21%), acute respiratory disease or infections (18%), neuro-psychotic episodes (6%), and sexually transmitted diseases (5%). Three street girls mentioned HIV/AIDS (children were allowed to mention more than one disease).

In order to know their health seeking behavior, we asked the children what they did when they got sick, where they sought treatment, how they paid for the cost of the treatment and the general problems they experienced with their ill health. Only about one third (37%) sought treatment from a health facility or social institution if they got sick. Twenty-eight percent looked for assistance from their friends and peers, and 13% stated that they waited to recover naturally. Another 33% treated themselves by buying drugs from dispensing stores. Only one quarter of the street children managed to get free health services from a public health facility. Most children stated that they were unwilling to seek treatment in a health facility because they did not have money to pay for the services. In-depth discussions in focus groups revealed that the health care personnel of most public health facilities that offer free services often behave in an unfriendly manner to street children. They yell at them and accuse them of being responsible for their own health problems. One street boy narrated his ordeal at a public hospital at Mnazi Mmoja:

> "I had been beaten severely by the mob in Kariakoo area for a crime I did not commit. They suspected me of having stolen someone's wallet and passed it to another boy who ran away. Some good people rescued me from this angry mob otherwise I would have died. When I went to the hospital to get treatment for my wounds, they asked me how I got them. After narrating the story, one nurse commented that it should be a lesson. I should not be surviving by stealing. The other one said, "They should have finished you completely. You street children are really a threat to our security in this city—particularly in the Kariakoo area."
> "With all these insults, they did not treat me. They said I should go to the police station and get a special form that will allow them to give me treatment. I left without medicine, and I did not want to go to the police

station, because I know the treatment will be sleeping in a police cell. Some of the wounds have healed naturally, but I am having problems with this one."(Street Boy aged 14 years).

The discussion ended with the boy showing us his oozing and badly swollen wound. We finally took him to a nearby clinic where his wound was cleaned and dressed.

6.4 Knowledge and Awareness of Sexually Transmitted Diseases

Health seeking behavior is not only a function of social and economic status and ability to pay. Knowledge, awareness and experience about disease can also influence a great deal how individuals seek health care. Our study was also interested in knowing whether children had knowledge about sexually transmitted diseases.

More than one half (56%) of the street children had some knowledge about STDs. Even after detailed explanations, 42% did not know what one meant by STDs. Of those who knew, 35% knew syphilis, 43% had ideas about gonorrhea, 49% had heard about HIV/AIDS and knew how it was transmitted from one person to the other. Only 29% knew fungus as a disease that can be transmitted sexually. There were significant differences between street boys and girls in terms of knowledge of STDs. While only 54% of street boys knew about some STDs, for the street girls, it was more than two thirds (69%). This is not surprising. The fact that survival sex is predominantly practiced more by street girls than street boys, makes it logical that street girls would have more knowledge about the dangers associated with sexual behavior.

In terms of STDs ever suffered, only 11% of street boys and 45% of street girls had ever suffered from a venereal disease. Again, survival sex as a coping strategy puts street girls in a much more vulnerable position than street boys. The children mentioned the STDs suffered as, syphilis (boys 2% vs. 14% for girls), gonorrhea (boys 5% vs. 20% for girls), HIV/AIDS (none for boys vs. 4% for girls) and fungus (boys 4% vs. 24% for girls). Fear of contamination from sexually transmitted diseases varies also by gender. About a one half of the street girls mentioned using condoms in sexual encounters in order to protect themselves from STDs. Only 14% abstained from any sexual encounters, and another 14% stated that they were in a hopeless and helpless situation and therefore did nothing to protect themselves. Only two girls mentioned taking medicine before sex, and only one took medicine after sex—a clear indication of ignorance on how STDs are transmitted. As for the boys, only 8% used condoms, 0.6% abstained from sex, 15% did nothing to protect themselves and only two boys took medicine before and after sex.

In their study of the sexual experience of the street children of Mwanza in Tanzania, Rajani and Kudrati (1996) confirm that street children are particularly at risk from infection with HIV and other sexually transmitted diseases for several reasons. These include the need to perform "survival sex" or prostitution, greater freedom to experiment with sex, and lack of adult protection and socialization. Rajani and Kudrati also noted that the incidence and recurrence of STDs were proportionally much higher in girls as compared to similarly physically mature boys.

Having sex at a tender age and with adult men has its own serious physical and psychological health consequences for street girls. Some of them may experience rough sex. As Schoepf (1997) has demonstrated, before menstruation begins, the lower reproductive tract is anatomically and physiologically immature and therefore vulnerable to tearing. The tearing of the vaginal lining can cause severe pain and trauma during sex and can create entry points for HIV (Lugalla 1999).

Olenja and Kimani (2000), in their study of prostitutes in Kisumu, in Kenya, narrate the episodes experienced by young girls in their pursuit for survival sex as follows:

"Given the tender age of the girls, they often referred to severe pain at sexual intercourse and after. Sometimes it takes a long time to recover. They experience severe backache/abdominal pain as well as pain in the genital area. One girl stated 'Because this man had paid for sex, I had to persevere whether or not it caused pain.' Thus child prostitutes experience generalized body aches due to excessive sexual activity with several partners whose body physiques differ markedly. Older prostitutes reported that they repeatedly face frequent abortions and sometimes infertility. Anal sex was said to be more lucrative compared to normal sex to the extent that when a client demands it most prostitutes would succumb to it even when it is not their general sexual orientation. Anal sex was reportedly the most uncomfortable type of sex especially among the younger prostitutes. They noted that those who practice anal sex have special problems. They suffer from anal itchiness and pain leading to extreme scratching and sometimes this causes infection. Over time the sphincter muscle loosens and fecal leakage becomes a common problem. To manage this, they put fresh garlic *kitunguu saumu* to cork up the anal exit to contain the leakage."

Although our findings suggest that most girls understand the health dangers associated with survival sex, it is still unclear as to whether the boys and girls consider the urban environment as a breeding ground for their ill health. This is evidenced by the fact that most children perceive their health status as good (67%). Only 26% considered their health as bad, and 8% didn't know. As reasons for their answers, those who thought that their health was good did so because they felt healthy, and those who thought their health was bad had experienced frequent and erratic episodes of illnesses. Only 5% knew about their health conditions after being informed by other people and particularly medical and health officials. There was no significant difference between boys and girls as far as these responses were concerned. The analysis stemming from these findings is that there is a close association between health seeking behavior and street children's perception of their own health. Street children are most likely not interested in seeking health care or being medically examined because, first, they perceive themselves as healthy individuals. Second, poverty hinders them. Third, they have negative attitudes towards health facilities because of the horrible treatment they experience. In this case, policy interventions that require street children to seek health care if in trouble will only bear positive results if they are accompanied by policies that advocate the improvement of patient-health personnel relationships.

Both boys and girls were interested in being medically examined, but only if, first, it were free of charge, and, second, that treatment would be available if they were found sick. These opinions featured most in focus group discussions in the following manner:

"They tell us to use condoms in sexual relationships, but where are they? If you go to places where they distribute them freely, sometimes you are told that if you are not more than 18 years old, you cannot get one. If you go to a drug store, they might be there but expensive." (Street boy aged 15 years)

"They also tell us to test our blood in order to know our HIV status. At the same time, they tell us that AIDS has no cure. If you get it you die. What is the logic of testing then? Is it for the purpose of letting you know that you are dying or what? Let death come on its own without my prior knowledge. It is painful to know that you will be dying soon."(Street girl aged 14 years)

In these statements, poor transmission of health messages is made clear. Swahili messages advocating "*Ukimwi Unaua*" (AIDS kills), "*Ukimwi hauna Dawa au Kinga*" (AIDS has no cure or prevention), which we usually hear on the radio, television and read in newspapers, are dangerous messages that are prone to misinterpretation. Health messages must be socially and culturally grounded. They must convey actual meanings, and different messages must address or target specific groups.

Most street children are not satisfied with the kind of life they experience. Their stories reflect a situation of despair, hopelessness and helplessness. They cite lack of parental care and love, lack of safety or security and difficulties involved in accessing basic necessities of life like food, shelter and clothing. Although they all agree that life is difficult in Dar-es-Salaam, it is evident from the findings of in-depth discussions in focus groups that they face these difficulties with courage because they consider their urban life to be an alternative or solution to the kind of life they confronted in the rural areas, where a bottle of beer is more easily found than a glass of clean water and death is a more common visitor than the medical doctor.

6.5 The Dar-es-Salaam Youth Health Clinic

In order to understand the magnitude of the health problems of street children of Dar-es-Salaam and to compare this magnitude with the information that we collected from street children themselves, we visited the Dar-es-Salaam Youth Health Clinic. This clinic was established in September 1995 in order to attract youths who were suffering from a variety of STDs, but feared to attend ordinary public health facilities because they would be seen by adult patients, some of whom could be their guardians, close relatives or even their parents (Chalamila 2000).

The clinic targets adolescents and youths below 24 years old, and its main objective is to provide reproductive health care. The main activities carried out by the clinic include (ibid):

- Management of Sexually Transmitted Disease cases.
- Screening Sexually Transmitted Diseases in order to detect infections in asymptomatic clients
- Individual and group counseling against STDs, drug abuse and alcohol indulgence.
- Initial support of family planning to sexually active youths who cannot refrain from sexual encounters.
- Provision of education on sexuality and reproductive health.

Since its establishment in 1995, the clinic has noted that most youths have limited information and skills for making responsible sexual decisions. As we argued earlier, young people lack easy access to appropriate information. About 60% of youths who attended the clinic in 1999 were ignorant about simple common features of their bodies and STDs. Twenty-two percent reported to have exchanged sex for money or materials. Thirty-eight percent had regular unprotected sexual intercourse, and 11% had started sexual activity as early as age 12 (Chalamila 2000). The data from the clinic reveals that 2% of males and 3.7% of females reported that they did not consent to the sexual act that ended up contaminating them with STDs.

The clinic served a total of 3,840 clients between August 1999 and July 2000. Of these, 158 were street children. Of the 3,840 clients, 55% were male and 45% were female. Their mean age at coitarche was 17 years for boys and 16.9 for girls. Fifty-nine percent of the boys and 22% of the girls had had more than 5 sexual partners since their coitarche. The overall rates of STDs recorded at the clinic were as follows: HIV infection was 7.2% in youths aged 10-19 years and 15.8% in those aged between 20-24 years. Eight percent of youths aged between 10-19 years had active syphilis, while for the 20-24 years age group, it was only 3.4%. Approximately 6% of the boys were HIV positive as opposed to 24% of the females (ibid).

Ninety-nine out of 158 (63%) street children tested positive for HIV. Of these, 36 or 36% stated that their sexual encounters were consensual, while 63 or 64% stated that their sexual encounters were forced (rape). Other STDs diagnosed from street children were genital discharge (37 boys vs. 15 girls) and genital ulcers (93 boys vs. 6 girls) (ibid).

The general analysis stemming out of the findings collected at the youth clinic suggests that adolescents and youths in Tanzania are increasingly becoming sexually active. The majority are, however, still ignorant about the consequences of their sexual activities. Most of them tend to practice unsafe sex, which leads to deleterious results on their health. The findings also show that sexual violence is rampant, particularly against street girls. If we collaborate the clinic's data of STDs suffered by youths and the 158 street children with our findings collected through the survey questionnaire of 403 street children and other ethnographic methods, the magnitude of health problems that street children experience in urban Tanzania is staggering.

6.6 Conclusion

It is evident from this chapter that street children live in an urban environment that is hard and puts street children in a vulnerable situation that affects their well-being. Because of the nature of street life, most children suffer from a variety of infectious diseases. Given their exposures to infections, road accidents, and violence and drugs—not to mention the noise, pollution, and blight of urban areas they inhabit—it is difficult to draw a picture of these children without an awareness of how their minds and bodies adapt to and cope with these adversities (Earls and Carlson 1999). The suffering of street children is not only physical but also mental (psychosocial). It is also clear that the coping strategies that street children develop in urban areas are gender specific. This reveals the importance of understanding gender differences in order to understand the fate of street children. Unlike boys, most girls practice survival sex. This survival strategy makes girls more vulnerable to contracting a variety of STDs than street boys. Our findings from the street children we interviewed and also from the Dar-es-Salaam Youth Clinic attest to this fact. More street girls suffer or have suffered from a variety of STDs than street boys. The information on street girls who are HIV positive is astonishing, proving that this survival strategy is quickly becoming a death strategy.

Having seen how serious the condition of street children is, one important question remains: What has gone wrong in Tanzanian families? What is the nature of the socialization of children, and how has it changed over a period of time? What is the relationship between the changing nature of family, the socialization process, and the increasing number of street children? Is there any relationship between the current crisis in the education system of Tanzania and the increase in number of street children? These questions are addressed in the next chapter.

Chapter 7

Social Change, Education and the Socialization of Children

7.1 Introduction

In the preceding chapters, we have demonstrated a variety of factors that push children into the streets. Poverty, abuses at home, and, in schools, the irrelevance of education have featured most in our discussion. We have also noted that most of the street children have hardly finished an elementary education. In this chapter, we want, first, to assess how processes of social change described already in chapter three have impacted traditional processes of socializing children, and the implication of this to the social welfare of children in Africa in general, but particularly in Tanzania. Second, taking into consideration the fact that the traditional system of socializing children has been replaced by a modern western system of education, we ask: what impact have the economic crisis and structural adjustment policies had on the system of education in Tanzania? What is the impact of the crisis in education on children's welfare? This kind of assessment is important because it opens up the relationship between methods of socializing children, their well-being and their role as young adult members of the society. We argue strongly that the changing nature of the African family has led to the changing nature of patterns of socialization. Values have been delocalized, and the community has been removed from being responsible for impacting norms and values of the society to the younger generation it has itself created. We also question the role played by the modern system of education in creating young adult members who are responsible and able to deal with problems that arise in their communities. We finally conclude that the withering away of the traditional patterns of socialization and the failure of the new modern methods of socialization are contributing to the growing number of children who live in conditions of hopelessness and helplessness.

7.2 The African Family and the African Child

As Kilbride and others have noted for Kenya, street children can be understood as one consequence of the rising culture of capitalism and the declining significance of African indigenous values, under which children were reared in strong family kinship units (Kilbride *et al.* 2001). In such extended families, both fathers and mothers were indispensable for the social and spiritual development of children (ibid.). Colonial as well as post-colonial social and economic policies have had severe consequences for the nature of the African family and how Africans perceive children and socialize them today. At the same time, the macro social and economic crises that Tanzania is experiencing have a greater impact at the micro level in general, but particularly at the family level. Due to increasing poverty, some parents, particularly fathers, desert their children and leave them under the care of their very poor mothers. In some families, poverty is forcing both the father and the mother to migrate to urban areas in search of wage employment. AIDS has also become the most notorious industry manufacturing powerless, orphaned children, most of whom can only depend on the sheer luck of community support in order to survive. At the same time, social and economic structures have broken down leading to a situation where social network support systems at community as well as at family levels are currently no longer in place. In traditional African extended families, it was not only the responsibility of the parents, but the entire community, to raise the children. The extended family, neighbors, friends, and other members of the society were equally responsible in socializing them. The children were the property of the whole community. Collective responsibility was especially prominent in the area of discipline, and any elder had the right to discipline a wayward child (Shorter and Onyancha 1999). Here, we adopt at length the analysis presented by Shorter and Onyancha (1999) exploring traditional forms of socializing children in Africa.

Children played an important role in marriages in traditional Africa. Usually, there was a procreative emphasis in marriage, and this emphasis pervaded the whole society (ibid). The transmission of human life was one of the more important, if not the most important, values of society (ibid). An individual was simply not alive if he/she was not engaged in transmitting life to another human being (ibid). Childless marriages were doomed to failure, barrenness was a stigma and arrangements were made to ensure that children were born in every marriage (ibid). Children were considered important in the society because they were a good source of cheap labor in a labor-intensive economy; they were also considered assets for future economic investment and life insurance for the parents when they became old. Because of these factors, most African families preferred having many children, thus making marriage and family central social institutions.

Because of the perceived positive role of children in society in traditional Africa, societies had specific formal and informal ways of training or socializing them so that they became responsible members of society. They were trained to grow into reproductive human beings, following the institutions and concepts of society Initiation into social maturity always included an initiation into sexual maturity with marriage in view (ibid). Such initiation had a strong emphasis on the body, the actual instrument by which one became a living, reproductive person (ibid). Both boys and

87

girls had to go through specific initiation ceremonies, and no one was allowed to marry before going through these rituals. The society sanctioned marriage, and all children were expected to grow and become both productive and reproductive members of the society.

Learning by doing was the most common method used in transmitting education and skills to the young generation. The children were prepared for family life by carrying out specific activities, assignments and responsibilities. As parents and elderly relatives aged or died, children took up their roles, most of which had been explained during initiation (ibid). The children were taught specific codes of social etiquette, particularly on matters relating to social behavior, social relationships with other people, taboos and sexuality (ibid). The children learned these values through direct interaction, observation, or traditional oral literature, songs and dances (ibid). As Shorter and Onyancha have argued, these values were strengthened through the formation of age-sets or groups of children who had been initiated together. These groups made sure that each member of the age-set followed the principles of behavior they had been taught by their elders. Anyone who broke the procedure would be ridiculed by the entire group, even punished and sometimes isolated. Since all members of the community were responsible in the socialization of children, this procedure helped to integrate the children and the community (ibid).

The advantage of this system of socialization is that children in difficult circumstances were not left to fend on their own; instead, they were helped. Orphans and illegitimate children were treated in the same way, and attempts were made by the entire community to make sure that all children were provided with security and protection. In case of the death of parents, relatives and grandparents assumed the responsibility of taking care of the orphans. Because procreation was of prime importance to the society, it only achieved its purpose when a child grew up and adopted appropriate adult roles and became a responsible member of the community (ibid).

7.3 The Impact of Social Changes on the African Family

In chapter three we have shown how processes of social change in Tanzania have had detrimental effects on children. The children have been affected greatly by these changes because the changes have had a severe negative impact on their families. Colonial and post-colonial politics and the impact of the structural adjustments have had negative consequences for the development of structures and institutions that held African societies together and helped the socialization of children. Land alienation and the introduction of a cash economy completely changed the nature of the African traditional economy. In places where people lost their land or had to use the small land left to them for both agricultural food and cash crop production, the foundation was laid for the development of rampant poverty, unequal development and social economic inequality. The introduction of a migrant labor system and taxation forced many men to migrate to urban or other rural places in search of employment opportunities. Most migrants left women and children at home, leaving all of the responsibility originally held by men to women. In some countries, it was not unusual for such male migrants to enter into casual unions with "host" women (ibid). Such unions contributed to the increase in illegitimate children, whose fathers evaded responsibility for their upbringing (ibid).

Overall, in Tanzania, there has been a large rise in the proportion of households headed by women—from 18% in 1991-92 to 23% in 2000-01 (HBS 2002). This is more pronounced in other urban areas than it is in Dar-es-Salaam. At the same time, it is evident that men are more likely to be educated than women in Tanzania. As poverty levels are strongly related to the education of the head of the household, one can understand what this means to children who remain under the care of their mothers only. A recent study has shown that 51% of individuals were poor if the head of the household had no education compared with only 12% when the head of the household was educated above a primary level (HBS 2002). This trend, which has been reinforced over recent years, has had a tremendous impact on children. It has meant that parents who lack the resources necessary to bring up their children are unwittingly condemning them to absolute poverty (ibid).

Today, increasing economic difficulties are leading to a situation where sharing and assistance within either the nuclear or extended family are becoming increasingly difficult. The traditional normal way of elder siblings assisting younger ones and employed relatives assisting the unemployed has disappeared. A study of orphans in Ileje shows that most orphans who turned to rural street life did so precisely because their relatives were not willing to take them in, or if they did, life was always characterized by economic difficulties, harassment, abuse and maltreatment. Sometimes such children have ended up being overworked and condemned almost to a slavery situation. These conditions and many others tend to force such children to opt for street life. Structural adjustments have increased economic difficulties in many households; most parents are now spending a lot of time sorting out appropriate ways of coping with poverty rather than thinking about socializing children. There is evidence from our focus group discussions of adults that economic difficulties at the household level generate multiple matrimonial problems. Migration is not the only factor creating single parents in rural areas, there are also other circumstances such as divorce, desertion, being widowed (particularly now as a result of AIDS) or simply not being able to find a partner to marry. Single women who have no economic

89

support face serious problems (ibid). As Shorter and Onyancha have observed for Kenya, the children of such women are deprived and are likely to migrate to the streets. Shorter and Onyancha also express the consequences of moral delocalization and its increase in pre-marital pregnancies, a phenomenon connected with unwanted children (ibid). Although statistics of teenage pregnancies in Tanzania are hard to come by, studies on AIDS and reproductive health reveal that teenage pregnancy is an increasingly serious problem in Tanzania (Kaaya *et al.* 1997).

Western systems of education have replaced the traditional education system, and sex education, which was common in traditional societies, is now disappearing. Western religious systems and morals consider traditional patterns of initiation and socialization to be immoral. Virginity, once an important value sought in those intending to get married, is currently considered something imposed by patriarchal social relations in order to control women's sexuality and, therefore, Western civilization has taken up arms to fight against it. The sex act itself, traditionally sacred and oriented towards procreation, has been trivialized (Shorter and Onyancha op.cit.). Foreign news networks do not simply promote free trade, political freedom, democracy and gender equality. Through movies, songs, comedies and drama, the message advocated is one of sexual freedom. Today, there is mounting evidence showing that teenagers in Tanzania become sexually active at a very tender age (Kaaya *et al.* 1997). Marriage has become increasingly unstable, and divorce, which was once frowned upon in African societies, is now a common occurrence (Shorter and Onyancha op.cit). Shorter and Onyancha have expressed the reasons behind this in the following way:

"Today, traditional reconciliation mechanisms are either unavailable or incompetent to deal with situations and problems of married people. For one thing, the communication aspect of marriage has diminished. Not only are the extended families less involved in the arrangement and celebration of marriages, but even the immediate parents have less and less say in the marriage of their own children. Many couples engage in open-ended relationships or trial marriages, and when it becomes apparent that the relationship is not working they separate. Some couples split up after a lengthy co-habitation. Others abandon the relationship in the face of economic problems." (Shorter and Onyancha op.cit.)

Shorter and Onyancha have argued that some street children reported to them that their parents simply deserted the family and that they had no idea where they were (ibid.). With the increasing situation of single parents who are mothers in Tanzania, there is no doubt that the observation noted in Kenya is equally true in Tanzania.

Leshabari (1996) has noted the lack of parental control over the behaviors of male youth among the Wanyakyusa in southern Tanzania because the traditional age-set structures that used to operate at village level are currently very weak because of the processes of social change. To some children, particularly girls, economic problems and other hardships are forcing them to become young wives. Some enter into "marriages of convenience" or sexual relationships with older men mainly for economic reasons and hence become vulnerable to the HIV infection.

Another trend linked to the changing nature of the African family is the collapse of traditional systems for resolving disputes at the local level. The role of elders in dealing with matrimonial disputes is increasingly becoming replaced by the modern Western judicial court system. In Tanzania, there is a provision for matrimonial problems to be settled by "reconciliation boards", but in practice these boards are male-dominated, gender-biased and ineffective. Divorce cases tend to be submitted directly to courts where divorces are granted without considering traditional norms and values, and in most cases, without due consideration of the impact of divorce on children. For example, according to Affiliation Ordinance Cap 378 of Tanzania, if the mother names somebody as the father of her child born out of wedlock and the court is satisfied on a balance of probabilities, the father is supposed to pay a maintenance allowance of not more than Tshs. 100 (equals 10 US Cents) per month or a lump sum of Tshs. 15,000 (US$ 20) only (URT Affiliation Ordinance Cap. 378). This legal amount of money is very small indeed and can hardly support the upkeep and welfare of any child. Due to this, courts have taken it upon themselves to adjust this amount according to the resources of the father and the prevailing economic conditions. But since this does not have legal backing, the father can at anytime challenge the amount imposed. The outcomes of modern judicial proceedings on divorce cases reveal that courts are more eager to dissolve relationships than they are to sort out ways of reconciliation (Shorter and Onyancha op.cit.).

With these trends, what we are observing is not only the collapse of the extended family and its related network of support, but also the increasing trend of single parents and the fracturing of the nuclear family across the African continent. The Household Budget Survey (2002) shows that there has been a decrease in household size from an average of 5.7 to 4.9 people between 1991 and 2001. There is also a small rise in the proportion of households headed by adults who are over 65 years old. Although this may be attributed to the decline in fertility, there are also reasons for us to believe that the AIDS epidemic is increasing the mortality rates of younger adults. It is very evident that the family as a basic unit of social organization and as an economic unit of society is now on the verge of collapse. Family stability and cooperation are disappearing with deleterious effects on children's welfare. As in

Kenya, children no longer belong to the community, and their life prospects and upbringing depend on the goodwill and integrity of individuals (Shorter and Onyancha op.cit.). At the same time, we must also acknowledge the fact that the increasing trend of single female parents reminds us that studies on the changing nature of the African family cannot be gender blind. If the traditional way of socializing children has been altered and replaced by the modern system of Western education, to what extent is the latter doing a good service to the children of Tanzania? This leads us to the discussion of the nature of education in Tanzania during the era of economic crisis and structural adjustment.

7.4 Education in the Era of Economic Crisis and Structural Adjustments

The economic crisis and the accompanying policies of structural adjustments (SAPs) have eroded enormously the achievements made by Tanzania from the late 1960s to 1970s in the area of education. While the number of children enrolled in school increased dramatically during this period--to a level of 98% for children of school-going age--due to a shortage of funds, the learning environment and quality of education the students received began to decline in early the 1980s—the early years of the economic crisis. The situation became much worse in the 1990s with the adoption of SAPs emphasizing a reduction of government expenditure in social services, and advocating cost-sharing or introducing user fees in these services, particularly in health and education.

A study by Kuleana (1999) has revealed that primary education is severely under-funded, poorly managed, and of extremely low quality. The results of a School Mapping Exercise in Kisarawe District in 1997 recorded the following:

- About 75% of 7 year olds have not been admitted to Standard One
- An average of 10% of pupils drop out of school every year for various reasons
- There is a constant decline in the number of pupils who are selected to join secondary education
- 13% of the pupils walk over 3 km to school
- There is a serious shortage of classrooms (56%) with a classroom-pupil ratio of 1:98 instead of the required 1:45. Consequently, 15% of classes are conducted under trees
- Many schools do not have permanent toilets. There is a shortage of 88% thus creating a ratio of 1:215 instead of the recommended 1:25.
- No schools have clean, safe water
- No school has a first aid box

- None of the 62 schools in the district have libraries, and 52% of the schools do not have bookstores
- Only 81 (19%) out of the 427 teachers have houses. Available houses are so dilapidated that they need major renovation
- 52% of the schools have no staff room
- There is uneven distribution of textbooks among wards and schools
- 40% of classrooms have no desks, thus forcing children to sit on the floor, logs, stones or even stand up throughout classes
- 280 out of 350 classrooms do not have blackboards. For demonstrations, teachers use pieces of hardboard and iron sheets that have not been painted black
- 79% of classrooms do not have teachers' tables and chairs
- None of these schools have started using the new curriculum developed in 1992
- There is a high rate of teacher absenteeism, meaning pupils lose many days of schooling
- 46% of the teachers hold 3 –B/C Grade. These teachers have primary school education. There is a surplus by 6% of teachers over and above the required number
- 50% of head teachers have a primary school education only
- None of the head teachers have been trained in school management
- There are no authentic data to show the district's allocation and expenditure on education

This is a common scenario in most schools in Tanzania. Even Tanzanian parents acknowledge this fact (see Table 8 below).

Table 8: Parental Attitudes Toward Education in Rural Tanzania in 1993 and 1997

Statement	Agree (%)	Disagree (%)	Don't Know (%)
Many parents would send their children to school if they thought their children would benefit	79 [82]	15 [14]	6 [3]
Children do not learn very much in primary school	58 [74]	31 [19]	11 [7]
Schools do not teach useful skills	60 [62]	33 [33]	7 [4]
Only rich people's children go to secondary school these days	72 [62]	25 [35]	3 [3]
The quality of education is improving	32 [28]	56 [61]	12 [11]

Source: Cooksey, Malekela and Lugalla, 1993:8; Cooksey and Mamuya, 1997a: Appendix II. Quoted from Kuleana 1999 page 6. The data not in brackets is for 1997 and the one in brackets is for 1993.

A Service Delivery Survey carried out by TADREG involving 2,588 respondents in 51 districts identified chronic problems that characterize the system of education in Tanzania as access, quality and participation (Cooksey and Mamuya 1997a, Kuleana 1999). Other studies have recorded similar findings or observations:

"It is not uncommon to find a teacher in front of 80-100 pupils who are sitting on a dirt floor without a roof, trying to convey orally the limited knowledge he has, and the pupils are trying to take notes on a piece of wrinkled paper using as a writing board the back of the pupil in front of him. There is no teacher guide for the teacher and no text book for the children" (Kuleana 1999 quoting Sumra 1995).

A study by Cooksey et al. (1993) quoted a mother from Kyela District as saying, "...all of my children have completed Standard Seven but none knows how to read and write" (Cooksey et al. 1993). With this in mind, the following statement can be recognized as a realistic assessment and not an exaggeration:

"The present education is not one to develop a person but rather a cunning way for some of the Ministry of Education workers to benefit themselves. The basic purpose of education is to provide light so that a person can get a good life. But nowadays nearly half the teachers are absent. They are out indulging in smuggling. The remainder are there at school taking it in turns to use the children as cheap labor" (Kuleana 1999 quoting Mabala and Kamazima 1996)

Due to the economic crisis and the implementation of SAPs, increasing enrollment in education has not been matched by a corresponding increase in funding to the education sector. For example, in 1996-97, the recurrent budget allocated only 14% to all types of education combined, as compared to 36% for debt servicing (World Bank 1997b, Kuleana 1999). The scenario is even more alarming if only basic education is taken into account: Tanzania spends fully four times as much on debt servicing as it does on primary education (Oxfam 1998a; Kuleana 1999). Lack of adequate funds for maintenance has led to a situation where infrastructure in most schools is dilapidated. Over 70% of school buildings have collapsing or leaking roofs, cracking walls and floors and no windows or lighting (Kuleana 1999). A study by UNICEF quoted by Kuleana (1999) claims that 80% of Tanzania's 3.7 million primary school students do not have desks, 30% of its over 100,000 teachers do not have a chair or desk and overcrowding is common. Many schools do not have clean water, and the state of sanitary facilities is particularly poor. Lack of water tends to have severe consequences on children's health. For menstruating girls, absenting themselves from school might be a rational decision in this kind of environment in order to keep themselves clean. Although official data shows that the toilet to pupil ratio is 1:68 in urban schools and 1:32 in rural areas, independent reports reveal a gloomier picture. A UNICEF study has noted that in Gwitiryo, there are only 4 toilets for 379 pupils and in Gitagasembe, there is just one for 234 pupils (Mabala and Kamazima 1996, Kuleana 1999). Once the former Minister of Education and Culture, Hon. Juma Kapuya was quoted as saying that only 40% of primary schools in the country had toilets, with the rest "doing it in the bush" (Kuleana 1999). A School Mapping Survey carried out in Kisarawe District in 1997 showed that there was one toilet for every 215 pupils (MOEC and UNICEF 1998).

Besides poor infrastructure, the quality of education is also determined by the nature of the curriculum, availability of teaching materials like books, quality teachers, teaching aids and methods. As Kuleana has argued, the state of each of these factors in Tanzania is a cause for concern. Lack of funding has forced teacher-training colleges to cut the teaching year by 20%, and many new teachers graduate without fulfilling the practical component (DANIDA 1996). A study by UNICEF has recorded the attitude of community members towards their teachers as follows:

"Many members of the community have little or no faith in the ability of the teachers of their children...in general parents have no faith in these UPE teachers". They do not see how a person who failed to go to secondary school can successfully educate another child."(Mabala and Kamazima, 1996).

It can come as no surprise that teachers' salaries are very low. A study by DANIDA (1996) reveals that in 1996, inflation-adjusted salaries for low-end teachers were 56% of 1977 salaries, and for higher-level teachers, they were a mere 20%. This means that despite increases in 1997, salaries have been falling in real terms. Some estimates reveal that teachers' salaries cover only about one third of living costs (Kuleana, 1999). Due to this, teachers moonlight in search of other sources of supplementing their incomes. Some reduce the number of teaching hours in order to spare extra energy for conducting extra paid tuition to their students. In some rural areas, teachers use their students as a source of income by making them work on their farms and other income generating projects during school hours without being paid. This situation, of course, reduces the morale of students and their desire to learn.

The curriculum in primary and secondary schools leaves much to be desired. Lack of required basic textbooks means that it is difficult for the teachers to implement adequately what is required in the curriculum. There are some subjects that are irrelevant to student's lives, do not focus on local problems and solutions and generally fail to teach students appropriate skills that can assist them in becoming self-reliant once they graduate from school. The general system of teaching is very authoritarian. Teachers control the classes and insist upon memorization. Little is done in order to encourage children's interest, creativity and participation (ibid).

Emphasis on practical skills is non-existent because students are evaluated by the quantitative data of examination results. President Benjamin Mkapa also raised concern in 1997 while touring a variety of district development projects. He criticized the heavy focus on examination scores only and emphasized the need for an education system that produces educated and socially developed human beings (*Daily News* September 23, 1997, Kuleana 1999).

In most schools, opportunities for participatory learning are hard to find. Curiosity and questioning are discouraged, and pupils rarely have the opportunity to be innovative, inquisitive or to think critically (ibid). In most schools in Tanzania, the teacher-student relationship is problematic and characterized by fear and mistrust. Corporal and other physical forms of punishment that can cause bodily injury are common. Sometimes these conditions scare the children, demoralize them and make them associate school with harassment, abuse, prison and torture. Some of them lose patience and decide to drop out from school and head for an alternative way of life in urban streets.

All these problems tend to have a variety of cumulative effects. Besides poor quality of education, they lead to a decline in enrollment rates. The enrollment rate of 98% of children eligible for primary education achieved during the UPE program in 1980 had declined to 71% just eight years later. UNICEF 1997 has noted that for every 100 children of primary school age, only 56 enroll in school. Of these 56 children enrolled in school, only 38 complete primary school. Of these 38 who complete primary school, only six proceed to secondary schools.

Official statistics from the Ministry of Education and Culture show that about one third of all pupils drop out from schools before they complete Standard Seven (MOEC 1998). The major reasons for school dropouts are higher school fees, irrelevant curriculum, dull and boring lessons, harassment and excessive punishment at school, poor infrastructure and ill-equipped classrooms. Other reasons are limited opportunity for secondary education, parents' and students' perceptions that the quality of education is declining, family poverty, hunger, pregnancy and lack of political will and commitment from the government to finance education adequately. The government's policy on education put an emphasis on parental responsibility for school expenses rather than a provision of free education for all. The 1997 TADREG Service Delivery Survey found that, in some regions, parents annually contributed an average of Tshs. 12,912 per pupil. Sometimes this amount went as high as Tshs. 30,000 for uniforms and various fees and contributions (Cooksey and Mamuya op.cit). This amount of money is considerably unaffordable to many people in both urban and rural areas. But legal enforcement makes sure that school fees are mandatory and paid. One letter from Serengeti District to the editor of *Msanii Afrika* claimed that parents' contributions were being collected using weapons such as bows and arrows (*Msanii Afrika* February 11, 1998, Kuleana op.cit). A study in Ileje District by Lugalla and Barongo (2000) shows that for poor families with many children, the cost of living is a serious burden that parents are unable to meet. As a result, some of them send their children across the border to schools in the neighboring country of Malawi where education is free and school uniforms are not enforced. What we learn here is that poverty contributes to low enrollment rates, later school enrollment (as parents try to postpone the economic burden) and a high incidence of pupils dropping out or having extended absences (Kuleana op.cit). Official statistics show that enrollment rates of school-age children in primary schools in Tanzania have substantially dropped from over 90% to approximately 75% since the introduction of the cost sharing exercise

97

(*Daily Mail* December 10, 1998). Recent data reveal that only 59% of 7-13 year olds were enrolled in primary schools in 2000-01 (HBS 2002).

In this study, we strongly agree with Kuleana's argument that, for the poor, the social and educational implications of mandatory cost sharing, in the absence of effective safety nets, can be enormous. The potential long-term effects may be very serious. Some of these effects include:

- Parents opting to remove children from schools or delay enrollment
- Children being beaten in school for non-payment of fees
- Children sent home and consequently missing many days of schooling
- Poor families decreased ability to allocate resources towards health and nutrition
- Large amount of teachers' time spent on collecting and managing fees
- Further erosion of relationship and trust between parents and schools/local authorities
- Equity severely undermined as the poor are increasingly unable to afford education

The remarks below from one parent in Mbeya confirm parent's dissatisfaction the whole idea of cost sharing:

> "We pay development levy. When we sell our crops we are taxed. We contribute to school buildings, and now they still want more money from us! We are not prepared to pay even a cent because they have got all our money with them. What are they doing with the money?" (Cooksey *et al.* 1993)

The other problem regarding education in Tanzania that has a direct impact on the welfare of children concerns the provision of education to children with disabilities. Article 23 of the Convention of the Right of the Child specifies the right of children with disabilities to special care, education and training in order to help them become self-reliant. The 1978 National Education Act section 56(1) promises that every citizen in United Republic of Tanzania shall be entitled to receive the level of national education that his ability will permit.

These promises have remained theoretical, and the actual practice reveals a different picture. There are only 16 special primary schools for children with disabilities in Tanzania. Of these, only 4 are for the blind, 7 for the deaf, 4 for the mentally disabled and only 1 for the physically disabled. Although attempts are made to integrate children with disabilities in ordinary schools, in practice, this policy is not producing good results. Hence, children with disabilities experience the most horrible form of discrimination in the Tanzanian education system. Our study has noted an increasing number of street children who are disabled and have never attended schools. We believe that these children are illiterate because they have been denied chances to get education due to these discriminative policies.

Another constraint in Tanzania's education system is gender inequity. Tanzania has been successful in addressing gender inequity in primary education as girls make up 49.6% of all children enrolled in primary schools. But enrollment of girls in secondary schools and schools of higher education is still problematic and very unequal. In 1997, girls made up only 46.6% of children entering Form One and just over one third (35.4%) of those entering high schools (Form Five). Overall, girls made up 45% of ordinary level secondary schools and 38% of higher secondary enrollment (Kuleana op.cit). But it is important to note that female dropout rates are higher in secondary schools. For the 1994-97-cohort group, 25% of the females dropped out as compared to only 15% of males (ibid). At the University level, gender enrollment disparities have remained skewed with no improvement in the past decade (ibid). In 1997-98, less than one fifth of total student enrollments at the University of Dar-es-Salaam were female, and approximately three times as many males were enrolled as females at the Muhimbili Medical School and Sokoine University of Agricultural Studies. At Open University, the female enrollment is only 12% of the total (ibid).

Good performance or achievement in education also depends on the nature of the learning environment. In Tanzania, as in many countries in Africa, the learning environment tends to be much less friendly to girls than to boys. By "learning environment" we mean parental and societal expectations, gender stereotyping in schools, sexual harassment and inadequate physical infrastructure. All these tend to promote lower female attendance and achievement. A study by Kuleana (op.cit) has described these problems in the following way:

"Many of the problems experienced in school such as late enrollment, and lack of water and sanitation facilities often have more serious implications for girls than for boys. Late enrollment for girls is particularly critical as a late school start takes them into puberty before completing Standard Seven. As the age for puberty rituals, early marriage and early pregnancy draws close, these girls are at increasing risk of dropout before finishing primary school. Similarly the lack of clean water to wash, inadequate toilet facilities, and in some cases lack of toilet doors may particularly affect girls during the time of their menstruation. The lack of privacy and unhygienic conditions may cause girls to stay home during this time, missing out on a number of school days each month."

99

There are other hidden forms of discrimination affecting females' ability to perform well in schools. These include erratic school attendance due to heavy workload in the domestic sphere. This may reduce the hours for doing private reading and homework. In brief, traditional practices tend to be biased against girls' education, and active participation by girls in school is discouraged by dominant patriarchal norms and values that tend to attach a stigma to women who are active, vocal and outspoken in public. These values associate women with the home and children, and not with the public sphere of life where prestige, wealth and power are exercised and achieved. Implicitly, these norms and values consider these privileges as the domain of men.

Our findings also reveal that poverty and education are intertwined. Using the mean monthly income per earner, the 2000-01 Household Budget Survey data show that the people with more education have higher average earnings than the least educated. Those with tertiary education earn 3.9 times more than what individuals with no education earn. These differences are larger in Dar-es-Salaam where earnings differ by a factor of 10 and are lowest in the rural areas (Table 9).

Table 9: Mean Monthly Income per Earner by Educational Level (TShs.)

Educational level	Dar-es- Salaam	Other Urban	Rural	Mainland Tanzania
None	17,901	20,815	16,732	17,007
Primary / adult education	57,296	45,390	25,079	28,669
Secondary	86,506	110,606	50,601	75,425
Tertiary	178,968	116,689	33,994	66,612
Total	69,038	51,163	22,660	27,463

Source: HBS 2002 page 82 (Table 9.5)

Table 10 and Figure 7 below show that incomes are skewed by gender. The men's average earnings are approximately 1.9 times higher than women's average earnings. These differences are larger in urban areas and smaller in rural areas (1.7 times that of women), particularly because there is a large pool of educated men with higher salaries. The other reasons accounting for this difference are the nature of participation in the labor market between sexes and the fact that, in general terms, men have higher levels of education than women and therefore are more likely to get waged employment that pays them well than their women counterparts.

Table 10: Mean Monthly Income per Earner by Sex (TShs.)

	Dar es Salaam	Other Urban	Rural	Mainland Tanzania
Male	96,069	73,406	29,212	36,758
Female	40,053	32,451	17,148	19,577
Total	69,038	51,163	22,660	27,463

Source: HBS 2002 page 83 (Table 9.6)

Figure 7: Mean Income per Earner by Sex and Educational Level ('000 TShs)

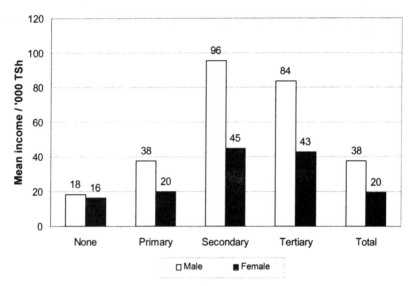

Source: HBS 2002 page 83 (Figure 9.1)

The above information warns us that when discussing poverty, education and income, there is a need to be gender conscious. The fact that sex differences in average earnings are larger in people who are more educated confirms that Tanzanian policies, laws and regulations are far behind in addressing gender inequality in the work place. It is clear that even in a situation where both men and women are highly educated and qualified, women are more likely to receive less pay for the same job than their male counterparts.

Information derived from the household survey also reveals that the people living in a household that has a head who has no education are over four times more likely to be poor than those in households whose head has education above primary level. Over one half of people from families headed by someone without any education are poor compared with only 12% households where the head has education above primary level (HBS 2002).

Table 11: Distribution of Poverty by Education Level of the Household Head

Educational level of the Head	HBS 1991/92		HBS 2000/01	
	Headcount ratio	% of the poor	Headcount ratio	% of the poor
None	45.6	32.2	51.1	36.9
Adult education only	51.0	9.8	46.4	5.2
Primary only	36.4	56.0	31.7	55.1
Above primary	13.2	2.1	12.4	2.8
Total	38.6	100	35.7	100

Source: HBS 2002 page 73 (Table 8.6)

Figure 8: Poverty Headcount by Education of the Household Head

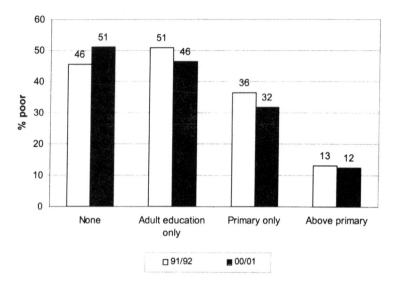

Source: HBS 2002 page 74 (Figure 8.1)

It is evident from the table and the figure above that those differences have grown wider since the early 1990s. These poverty levels have increased for the households that do not have educated heads and have declined significantly for other groups. The percentage of poor heads of households without education increased from 32% to 37% between 1991-92 and 2000-01, while that of households with education above primary level went up from 21% to 28% during the same period. There is also evidence that the poor are less likely to send their children to schools than those who are relatively not poor. Data from the Household Budget Survey (2002) reveals that two thirds of children aged 7-13 years in poor households were attending school by 2001 compared with only 50% of children living in the poorest households.

104

Figure 9: Percentage of Children Studying by Poverty Status and Year

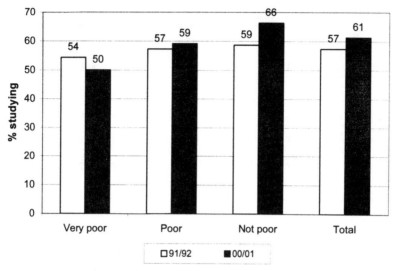

Source: HBS 2002 page 75 (Figure 8.3)

As the data from the figure above shows, it is obvious that school enrollments for children from very poor families have declined progressively over the 1990s from 54% to 50% and have increased slightly for the poor and those who are not in poverty. Since Tanzania introduced cost-sharing policies in education in the early 1990s, there is every reason to believe that the declining school enrollment figures for children from very poor families reflect the inability to afford the cost of education, a consequence of structural adjustment. Although the decline in enrollment figures is recorded in both rural and urban areas, in-depth studies show that the rural poor have fallen further behind than the urban poor.

Table 12: Percent of Children Aged 7-13 Years who are Studying by Poverty Status

	1991/92			2000/01		
	Very poor	Poor	Non- poor	Very poor	Poor	Non- poor
Total	54.4	57.3	58.6	50.1	59.2	66.3
Dar es Salaam	59.2	69.7	66.1	56.3	69.6	79.9
Other urban	57.4	65.7	64.9	60.2	68.1	81.9
Rural	53.9	55.7	56.9	48.8	57.7	62.2

Source: HBS 2002 page 76 (Table 8.8)

When this is examined in the context of increasing poverty in rural Tanzania, it becomes clear why many rural youths who are uneducated migrate to cities in search of an alternative life style. Since they lack appropriate paper qualifications, it becomes difficult for them to compete successfully in an urban open labor market that values people with school certificates. Due to the close association between poverty and education, one scenario that is clear is that children from very poor families are likely to become very poor and uneducated youths and eventually very poor, uneducated parents themselves. And, thus, we see a vicious cycle of poverty for future generations. Targeting such marginalized social groups should always be the mission of any responsible and accountable government.

7.5. Conclusion

This chapter has shown how the processes of social change that have taken place in Tanzania have changed the nature of family, and how this has changed both the nature and pattern of socializing children. The traditional belief that "It takes the entire village or community to raise a child" is no longer so. Children are no longer part of the community, and what they learn from modern schools has no relationship to their local problems and needs. The traditional pattern of socialization has been turned upside down, and children of today have difficulty assuming responsibilities and adult roles in their communities when their parents get old. We have also shown how the new system of socializing children through schools is not producing good results.

Besides the fact that what is being taught is irrelevant, the quality of teaching itself leaves much to be desired. Fear, rote repetition and boredom characterize the curriculum and students' negative responses to it (Kuleana op.cit). The relationship between parents and teachers and teachers and children is characterized by enmity. Parents hardly know what is happening in schools and basic materials, such as stationery for progress reports so parents know how their children are progressing, are nonexistent. In a study of Cooksey, Malekela and Lugalla (1993), one parent from Ngara District voiced his concern in the following way: "In the previous times, teachers were a shining example in the whole village. In their leisure time they used to visit us in our homes, which brought contact and an opportunity to discuss our children's behavior. Today this is no longer so."

The cost of education is increasingly expensive, and the government is placing the burden of financing education on parents, most of whom are poor and cannot afford such fees. This is leading to a situation where the children of the affluent social classes receive quality education in private schools or abroad, while the children of the poor continue to receive mediocre education or lack even the chance of accessing this mediocre education. This situation undermines the potential for the development of democratic citizenship and constitutes a violation of a basic right of all children (Kuleana op.cit) The problems experienced in education contribute a great deal to pushing children into streets. Hostile environments in schools, authoritarian school leadership, lack of participation by parents and students in school affairs and excessive physical punishments lead to dropouts and force some children to migrate to cities. We have also shown that the education system is very discriminative toward children with disabilities, and such children from poor families are likely to migrate to cities where they cannot get employment but can survive by begging. What is evident from this chapter is that any improvement in the pattern of socialization of children, whether through schools or communities, can have a positive impact on the welfare of children. It is very likely that it can reduce the number of young children drifting to towns in search of alternate ways of life. Education of high quality that imparts productive skills is crucial to the production of self-reliant, responsible citizens. It is also important to increase opportunities for secondary education so that young boys and girls who are not yet mature enough to lead an independent life can continue schooling.

It is also evident from the findings of this study that women play a vital role in raising children in the Tanzanian society. The Swahili proverb that says *"Ukimuelimisha Mwanamke Umeelimisha Taifa Zima"* ("By educating a woman you educate the entire nation") teaches a fundamental lesson. However, what this chapter has revealed is that women are being discriminated against in education and employment opportunities. There are deliberate policies that hamper them from accessing the resources of wealth, power and prestige. Their domain is still in the domestic sphere of life, but even here it is unlikely that they have full control over the products of their labor for their own benefit. Implementing policies that focus on empowering and emancipating women can be of great help in the welfare and socialization of the children of Tanzania.

If the traditional system of socializing children has collapsed and the new system of education is failing to perform its role, and if all of these tend to increase the number of street children, we need to assess how the government is reacting to this situation. If it has failed to address the falling standards of education, is the Tanzanian government properly addressing the street children problem? What policies has the government adopted? Are these policies working? These issues are examined in chapter eight.

Chapter 8

The State's Policy and Street Children

8.1. Introduction

How the state and the general public perceive street children will certainly influence both the kind of policies adopted by the state in order to solve this problem and the ways in which the public in general will react to the problem and design measures to address it. How the state and the public perceive street children also influences how the children perceive themselves and how they evaluate themselves in relation to other members of their society. In this chapter, we attempt to examine the relationship between the state and street children. We do this by examining the kind of policies that the state has adopted in order to address these issues. We finally identify the major weaknesses that are inherent in state policies and provide suggestions on how to improve them.

8.2. The State and Street Children

How the state reacts toward the problem of street children has to be seen within the context of its attitude toward poverty in general and particularly the urban poor. The position of the government on the situation of street children is ambivalent. First, there are officials who think that street children are a pathological urban cancer. They regard them as unemployed loafers, abandoned, young criminals, thieves and prostitutes destined to become hard-core criminals and gangsters in the future. Those who look at them in this way strongly believe that street children must be removed from urban areas. They believe that cities would be better and cleaner if street children no longer existed.

The second viewpoint perceives street children as young people in difficult circumstances who have for some reason left or been abandoned by their families and are now struggling on their own to survive. They consider them well-organized and very rational when making decisions about how to pursue survival, and they understand that sometimes the harsh conditions of urban life and the necessity to survive force these children to break laws. The policy recommendations that flow from this perspective are dramatically different from those who fear and aim to punish these children. Instead of removing children from the streets forcibly, this sympathetic outlook encourages official policies to protect them and to assist them so that they can live normal, decent lives. Such positive outcomes are possible with the provision of security, shelter, clothing, housing, health care, education and vocational training from sympathetic adults. Where possible, and through vigorous counseling, attempts should be made to reunite these children with their families.

The third viewpoint looks at the street children as an inevitable outcome of uncontrolled capitalist development (globalization) in an underdeveloped economy. It is an unfortunate consequence of the globalization process as it intensifies poverty, destroys communities and dismantles families. The persistence of rural poverty, the impact of matrimonial conflicts and abuse and now the AIDS epidemic are problems that are growing quickly in Tanzania due to specific processes of social change and development. Those who adopt this viewpoint take a paternalistic view toward street children. They consider street children as unfortunate, poor individuals who require assistance from other people who are more fortunate and wealthy. In terms of policies, this approach does not differ with proposals by those who hold the second viewpoint. But in some cases, those who hold this viewpoint have radical ideas about how to change the situation in that they believe that justice and welfare for marginalized social groups can only triumph once the entire system that promotes poverty and social inequality is overhauled.

Our experience of Tanzania shows that the first perspective dominates. We have continually witnessed police brutality towards street girls who practice commercial sex (*Changu-Doa*). Cases of these girls being arrested, beaten and sometimes abused by the police themselves are common. We often see street boys and beggars being arrested by the city officials and repatriated to their rural home areas. These examples confirm that the position of the government toward street children and the urban poor in general is negative. The attitude of government officials toward street children is, in short, a reflection of how the state in Tanzania evaluates the urban poor. Again, there are three main positions held by different policy planners. First, there are those who look at poverty in terms of poverty itself. These argue that the poor are responsible for their own situation. They are seen as an urban social cancer that has penetrated and therefore, must be eliminated.

The second view looks at the urban poor as victims of social, economic, and political circumstances. These are people in horrible conditions, and what they need from both the state and the public is sympathy and moral and material assistance. Those with these views attempt to suggest policies that seek to improve the welfare of the urban poor. Most of the NGOs that provide services to street children are a result of this way of thinking.

The third view looks at the urban poor as innocent individuals who are a product of the social system. It is the social system that is responsible for their misery. Those who think along these lines agree that existing social and economic policies have created processes of social economic inequalities. These processes breed rampant social injustice and manufacture a situation of hopelessness and powerlessness for some, while at the same time, enriching a few segments of the society at the expense of the marginalized poor. These views tend to produce radical policies that seek to address the essential relations rather than phenomenal forms. According to those who hold these views, justice and the welfare of the majority can only become a reality if the entire system is overhauled and equal opportunities exist for all people to access resources of wealth, power and prestige.

At an International Conference on Street Children and Street Children's Health that we organized and convened in April 2000 in Dar-es-Salaam, two honored guests from the government were invited in order to officiate the opening and closing ceremonies. The Director of Women and Children in the Ministry of Community Development, Women Affairs and Children gave an opening speech, and the Commissioner of Social Welfare from the Ministry of Labor and Youth officiated the closing ceremony. We decided to invite these key people from the government because their Ministries, and particularly their departments, are directly responsible for formulating policies and charting effective strategies aimed at dealing with the problems that confront street children.

In her speech, the Director of Women and Children argued that it was important to look at the problem of street children not in isolation from the other problems facing the Tanzanian society as a whole. She said, "Street children are a manifestation of societal problems often rooted in the prevailing social economic and political situations of our countries" (Mangeesho 2000). She argued that a holistic approach is necessary if one is interested in searching for long-term solutions to the problem.

The Director said that the government's sectoral ministries, which are responsible for children and social welfare in collaboration with relevant institutions, NGOs and civil society, have instituted policy measures to ensure the survival, development and protection of children as well as strategies aimed at creating a conducive environment for all those who care for children, including those in need of special protection measures. She emphasized that the task of caring for children is primarily the responsibility of parents and society at the family level. She also pointed out that unless poverty is eradicated, the problem of street children will certainly continue (ibid).

In his closing speech, the Commissioner for Social Welfare pointed out that children are the potential leaders of Tanzania. However, he cautioned that this was bound not to happen if the children continued to be affected by a variety of problems like truancy, drug abuse, delinquency, sexual harassment and abuse, emotional imbalance, poor health and lack of self direction. He argued that the whole society is responsible for this anomaly (Kameeka, 2000).

There is no doubt that the messages from the Director and the Commissioner were strong and reflected the reality of this problem and how the government conceptualized it. However, what is needed is not only a conceptualization of the problem, but also the designing of appropriate policies accompanied by effective strategies of implementation. In order to understand whether this is happening in Tanzania, we need to examine the recent government policy on child development.

Tanzania is a signatory of the Convention on the Right of the Child. By signing this convention, Tanzania has accepted that the rights of the child as stipulated in the convention. These include; (i) Survival rights, (ii) Developmental rights (iii) Protection rights (iv) Participation rights, and (v) The right not to be discriminated against. In order to implement these objectives, Tanzania has been obligated to design a Child Development Policy, the objectives of which are: (Child Development Policy of Tanzania 1996).

- To define a child in the Tanzanian context
- To educate the community on the basic rights of a child
- To provide direction and guidance on child survival, protection and development
- To provide direction on the upbringing of children in difficult circumstances
- To enable the community to understand the source of problems facing children
- To give proper direction to children, so that they may become good citizens
- To clarify the role and responsibilities of children, parents, guardians, community, institutions and the government in planning, coordinating and implementing plans for children
- To emphasize the joint responsibilities of both parents (men and women) in caring for and bringing up their children
- To educate the community in order to ensure that children inherit good traditions and customs
- To ensure that there are laws which can be used to deal with child abuse

The Policy became operational in 1996. It gave direction on how to protect and defend children's rights, and also gave direction to different institutions on how to implement effectively the United Nations Convention on the Right of the Child. Although the policy objectives are appealing, it is not clear as to how they will be implemented. The other major weakness of the policy is that it lumps all children into one group. There is no attempt to acknowledge the fact that children are not the same. There are those who originate from relatively wealthy families and middle-income families, and those who come from desperate, very poor families. On the one hand, there are children who live alone in the streets, disadvantaged, and on the other hand, there are those who come from families where they are being abused. As we will demonstrate below,

112

the policy has failed to address the ambivalent nature of the definition of a child in Tanzania.

Since the policy began operating, a variety of new developments have taken place in Tanzania. The rapid increase of HIV/AIDS has increased the number of orphans, an issue which was not taken into consideration when the policy was being designed. The other issue is the increasing situation of poverty in rural and urban areas and the negative impact of structural adjustment policies. These social processes have simultaneously contributed to the collapse of families, extended family networks and communities. These problems and others have produced conditions that generate children who live in situations of helplessness and hopelessness. The rapid increase of street children in urban Tanzania during the last 10-15 years is a result of these processes.

8.3 Tanzania's Legal Regime and Children's Rights

In virtually all the societies of traditional Africa, children's rights and privileges were favorably articulated within the family community. Every society prescribed patterns of behavior and customary conduct to both parents and children. On the one hand, parents were expected to monitor, feed, clothe, protect and educate children. Children, on the other hand, were expected to obey and respect their parents. A system of checks and balances was thus established which gave stability to society (Shorter and Onyancha 1999).

As we have documented in other chapters, the family in Tanzania is changing quite considerably, and this change is impacting children's rights heavily. The legal regime of Tanzania does not render enough protection to children, let alone to street children. The law lumps together street children and other children without taking into account the fact that street children are, in fact, a disadvantaged group who suffer double jeopardy, first as children, and secondly as street children.

Presently, the definition of who is a child in Tanzania is still vague and problematic. The law governing children's rights and by extension, street children's rights, is fragmented and scattered in different pieces of legislation that are sometimes contradictory. Mbunda (2002) has noted that the word "child" or "young person" has no uniform definition. Various pieces of legislation define a "child" or a "young person" by using different ages in order to serve a specific purpose of that legislation.

According to Mbunda (ibid), the constitution of the United Republic of Tanzania of 1977 allows anyone who has reached the age of 18 to seek any leadership post. "The Age of Majority Ordinance Chapter 431" defines an adult person as one who is 18 years old. The Interpretation of General Clauses Act, 1972, defines a child as one who has not reached the age of 18 years. This age limit is also indicated in the

"Registration of Births and Deaths Ordinance Cap. 108" and "Sexual Offences (Special Provisions) Act 1998". The "Adolescence Ordinance Cap. 355" defines a child as one who is below 21 years old, and the "Employment Ordinance Act, Cap 336" considers a child as one who is below 15 years, and a youth as one who is 15 years old or above but is not yet 18 years old. At the same time, the "Children and Young Persons Ordinance Cap 13" regards a person who is below 12 years as a child and a person between 12 and 16 years as a youth. "The Penal Code Chapter 16" stipulates clearly that any child who has not reached 10 years cannot be prosecuted for any offence, and the Education Act of 1978 says that a child is any person who is between 7 and 18 years old.

It is evident from the above exposition that the definition of a child or a young person in the legal system of Tanzania has never been unanimous, but rather contextual (Mbunda 2002). This weakness has led to a situation where, first, the legal system of Tanzania is having difficulties in protecting children's rights, and, second, the government is having trouble setting out a clear child development policy that does not look at children or youth as a homogenous group.

Section 176 of the Penal Code deals with what the law terms "Idle and Disorderly Persons." The section identifies seven categories of persons who are defined and deemed by the law to be "idle and disorderly persons." Always, these are prostitutes, beggars, gamblers, pimps, and others who fall into related groups. These seven categories are (Lugalla 1995):

- Every common prostitute behaving in a disorderly or indecent manner in any public place or loitering or soliciting in any public place for the purpose of prostitution
- Every person wandering or placing himself in any public places to beg or gather alms, or encouraging or forcing any child or children to do so
- Every person playing at any games of chance for money or money's worth in a public place
- Every person wandering abroad or endeavoring to obtain or gather alms by exposure of wounds or deformation
- Every person who publicly conducts himself in a manner likely to cause a breach of the peace
- Every person who, without lawful excuse, publicly does any indecent act; and
- Every person who in any public place solicits for immoral purposes

Section 177 states that anyone who is convicted twice of the above offenses under section 176 is deemed to be "a rogue and a vagabond," and is eligible on the first offense to an imprisonment of three months (without the option of a fine), and for a subsequent offense, to an imprisonment of one year.

The Written Law (Miscellaneous Amendments) (No. 2) Act of 1983, among other things, amends the Penal Code (Chapter 16 of the Laws) section 176 by adding two more categories to the already existing seven categories of idle and disorderly persons. They are:

- Any able-bodied person who is not engaged in any productive work and has no visible means of subsistence

- Any person lawfully employed who is, without any lawful excuse, found engaging in personal entertainment at a time when he is supposed to be at work.

To whom does the eighth category refer? Basically, these are people who are unemployed and actively yet unsuccessfully seeking work. According to this law, they are criminals and are therefore subject to either a fine of 500 Tshs. or three months in prison or both. This also includes workers who have been labeled as unneeded and thrown out on the streets through no fault of their own. Clearly, there is no attempt to see the unemployed as victims of the social and economic system as a whole.

The Legal Aid Committee of the Faculty of Law at the University of Dar-es-Salaam has argued that, under this law, the unemployed are being punished twice. First, they are punished by being deprived of the employment through which they would earn their living and, second, by being made criminally liable for that state of unemployment. The committee argues further that:

"Politically, it is adding insult to injury to lump a section of the working class together with gamblers and pimps. Legally, it is a grave folly and an act of desperation to believe that social and criminalizing them can solve economic problems like unemployment. This is besides the insurmountable problems of enforcing such a law and giving a fair and just interpretation of such terms as 'productive work', and 'visible means of subsistence."

Street children and other jobless youth always suffer from these discriminating and violent laws. The above confirms that, in terms of political practice, Tanzania does not respect the articles of the Convention of the Right of the Child of which it is a signatory. This convention was adopted by the United Nations General Assembly on November 20, 1989, and began operating in September 1990. The convention comprises various categories of children's rights, particularly survival, developmental, protection, and participation (Shorter and Onyancha 1999, United Nations Convention on the Right of Child 1991).

The right to survival means that every child has the right to life. In this case, the right to survival—Article 6(1)—means the provision of adequate food, shelter, clean water and primary health. The right to development—Article 6(2)—requires the signatories of this convention to ensure that children survive and develop. These rights include access to information, education, cultural activities, and opportunities for rest, play and leisure, and the right to freedom of thought, conscience and religion (Shorter and Onyancha 1999). The right to protection (Article 16) makes sure that children are protected from interference with privacy, the family, the home and correspondence. The child should also be protected from all forms of exploitation and cruelty and arbitrary separation from the family and also from abuses in the judicial and penal systems (ibid). Article 12, which gives children the right to participation, is aimed at making sure that the children are able to express their opinions and that their views are seriously considered. Children are also supposed to play an active role in the community and society through freedom of association (ibid).

These rights can be enforced in each country only if they are incorporated in policies aimed at protecting and developing children and, also, if they are included in the legal regimes. As we have already demonstrated, Tanzania is far from achieving this since even the definition of a child is still contextual and problematic. Even the Child Development Policy itself, which was introduced in 1996, is now being redrafted, and it is unclear as to when the new one will become effective. The definition of who is a minor, juvenile or a young person remains ambiguous and tends to predispose children to vulnerable situations where they can be easily abused.

We have seen that laws that criminalize loiterers have always ended up abusing and mistreating street children. The news below reported by *Nipashe* newspaper confirms this kind of harassment.

"Nineteen youth below the age of 18 were on 28th were sentenced by the court to be canned or pay a fine of Tshs.2000 ($ 2.50) after pleading guilty to a "crime" of disturbing passengers at the Dar-es-Salaam's main bus terminal. The prosecutor argued before the court that the youth had been operating small businesses illegally in the bus terminal area, and have been disturbing passengers by making a lot of noise." (*Nipashe* March 29, 2001)

This is a clear example of how authority tends to exercise abuse against the children it is supposed to protect. Law enforcement and urban authorities consider street children to be a menace to the city. They are invariably seen as people who commit crime, thereby inflaming desires to see them eliminated from the urban environment. They are branded with names like "*Wadokozi*" or "*Wachomoaji,*" "V*ibaka*" (pickpockets, thieves), or "*Wahuni*" (hooligans) (Lugalla 1995, Lugalla and Mbwambo 1999). According to section 176 of the Penal Code of Tanzania, street children are considered to be "Idle and Disorderly Persons" and therefore subject to criminalization (ibid).

However, in-depth studies on street children reveal a different picture. Studies by Rajani and Kudrati (1996) and Lugalla and Mbwambo (1999) show that street children are more down to earth in terms of their survival strategies and are capable of evaluating themselves. They normally describe themselves as "*Watemi, magangwe*" or "*watoto wa maskani*" or "*mtaani*", meaning tough, very strong, carefree people who hang out. Others call themselves as "Born-Town," or "Born-Here-Here," indicating that they are a product of the social system itself and are therefore familiar with and used to this "horrible" life.

Due to the fact that the state and the public tend to look at street children in a negative light, frequent arrests and violent conflicts between street children and other members of the society are not hard to see. As our earlier findings reveal, most street children know very well what a police cell looks like. They are constantly arrested and accused of stealing, pick pocketing and loitering. There is clear evidence from in-depth discussion in focus groups that street children evaluate the police as enemies of the society rather than as security overseers. Due to this, street children are less likely to go to the police to report episodes of discrimination, harassment and abuse from other members of the society. According to them, going to the police to report such episodes amounts to turning yourself in. In brief, as Shorter and Onyancha (op.cit) have argued for Kenya, the law in Tanzania does not protect street children; rather, it labels them as criminals. As a result, those who molest street children--perpetrators of mob justice--are never arrested and prosecuted. Sometimes they continue abusing street children with the help of law enforcement institutions.

What the government seems to forget is the fact that street children are "neglected children". On the one hand, their own families have neglected them. They have been denied of the parental love, care and protection. On the other hand, the government, by not introducing social policies and infrastructure that assist children in difficult circumstances, is also neglecting street children. Street children lack access to the education and health services that are enjoyed by an ordinary child in a family setting.

In brief, what we see is a situation where all rights of the child as stipulated in the Convention of the Right of the Child are neglected in Tanzania. Most laws relating to children tend to act against street children instead of protecting them. Street children live in an environment where they cannot enjoy the privileges associated with childhood. Street children tend to take up adult roles at a very young age and, for this reason, they are in most cases treated as adults.

8.4 Conclusion

It is clear in this chapter that the government is lacking a clear policy aimed at addressing a variety of problems that poor urban children in general, and particularly street children, experience. The Child Development Policy that has been operational since 1996 is very weak, and simply accommodates what the Convention of the Right of the Child stipulates, but does not show the steps that must be put into practice in order to implement the objectives of the convention. No attempt has been made so far to enforce the objectives of the convention through legislation. Due to this, children in general are lacking full protection in Tanzania. The street children are experiencing a double jeopardy, first, as children, and second, as street children. The definition of "Who is a Child?" in Tanzania is vague, ambivalent and contextual. And we strongly believe that unless there is a clear definition of a child in Tanzania, all other policies that seek to protect and improve the welfare of poor children are unlikely to be successful. The findings of this study show that children in Tanzania are not a homogenous entity. Policies that do not acknowledge this reality miss the target group. Tanzania has left the entire responsibility of dealing with street children to the civil society. At present, the number of NGOs being established in order to address this problem is overwhelming. What are these NGOs doing? Are their activities going to solve this problem? How can the services of street children NGOs be improved? We attempt to address these questions in chapter nine.

Chapter 9

The Civil Society and the Welfare of Street Children

9.1 Introduction

In the previous chapter, we examined the position of the state vis-à-vis street children in Tanzania. We also assessed the kind of policies that the government has adopted in order to improve the welfare of children in general. We have noted that, the government does not have a policy that attempts to look into problems that street children experience. In reality, the civil society, through a variety of non-governmental organizations (NGOs), is doing a great deal more to assist street children in Tanzania than the state is. Since NGOs are involved in practice, it is important to understand the nature of the street children NGOs in order to understand the kind of activities they are engaged in, their achievements and problems, and the ways in which their services can be improved. In view of this, we invited some NGO leaders to our conference in Dar-es-Salaam, so that they could present their candid experiences of working with street children. During the two-year period of this study, we also managed to visit a total of 35 street children NGOs that work in ten major urban centers of Tanzania. Therefore, the material presented below reflects our perceptions of the thirty-five NGOs we visited and our analysis of the interviews we had with some leaders of the NGOs during the conference.

The services that these organizations offer to street children are as varied as the organizations themselves. In this chapter, we present a thorough analysis of these NGOs by discussing their types, the kind of philosophies they represent and the type of support they provide to street children. We assess their levels of success; both in terms of their own goals and philosophies, and also in terms of whether the services they offer provide a long-term solution to the problem of street children. We also discuss their major weaknesses and the problems that they confront in providing these services. Finally, we suggest ways of improving their services.

9.2 Nature of Street Children NGOs

Most street children NGOs were established over the past decade. Our study has noted that almost all NGOs began their activities in the early and mid 1990s. There are several explanations for this. First, studies of street children in Tanzania link the rapid increasing rate of street children in Tanzania with the increasing rate of poverty, and the 1990s have been bad years for Tanzania as far as economic development is concerned. Second, the economic crisis, which began in early 1980s, intensified in the 1990s. Thirdly, the policies of Structural Adjustments propagated by the World Bank and IMF that were adopted by the government in mid 1980s began showing their negative impact on the lives of the majority Tanzanians in the 1990s. The net result of all this is the fact that Tanzania has witnessed the destruction of family and community social support structures, a situation that has led to the rapid production street children during the last few years.

While poverty has been intensifying, the ability of the government to address the growing social development problems has been declining. As a result, what has happened during the last 10-15 years is the presence of what one would call a "development space." This space has to be seen in terms of the inability of the government to play its role as a facilitator of social development. In order to fill this space, the development of civil society associations became necessary. In fact, the mushrooming of NGOs and Community Based Organizations (CBOs) in Tanzania during this period reflects the failure of the government to play its role as a facilitator and promoter of development. It is therefore important to understand the development of street children NGOs within this context. These NGOs have increased tremendously during the last few years in order to address the problem of the increasing rate of unsupervised children living alone in the streets of urban Tanzania after noting the government's inactivity and seeming disinterest in the solving the problem.

An analysis of the NGOs and projects we visited reveals that these NGOs are varied in nature. Approximately one third are charity religious-based NGOs owned by either the Catholic or the Protestant Churches. Others are non-denominational. Some of the NGOs are not NGOs par excellence, but rather special projects operating under the umbrella of a major organization. For example, the Iwambi Street Children Project of Mbeya and the Huruma Street Children in Iringa are projects that operate under the respective Dioceses of the Evangelical Lutheran Church of Tanzania. The Faraja Street Children Project in Iringa and the Upendo Children's Home in Moshi are under the umbrella of the Catholic Church. The Lighthouse Street Children Project in Arusha operates under the umbrella of the Global Concert Ministry.

Most of the NGOs provide services to street boys only. Only 11 organizations provide services to both boys and girls. And, in fact, the number of girls in these organizations was very minimal. Those that provided services to both sexes had no more than 5 girls in their respective centers. Kwetu Counseling Center of Dar es Salaam was the only organization that provided services to street girls only. The fact that many NGOs serve only boys does not mean that there are no street girls who would like to enjoy their services. As our findings have demonstrated, one important

120

factor is that street girls are highly invisible in streets. Pimps take most of them immediately upon finding them in the streets, so that they can operate in the commercial sex business. Others are easily absorbed in households as domestic servants. Most leaders of several NGOs argued that they did not want to work with street girls because of their vulnerability to becoming pregnant, a potential situation that would necessitate assisting both the girls and their street babies.

9.3 Services of Street Children's NGOs

Street children NGOs and projects attempt to deal with a variety of problems that children in difficult circumstances experience. Some of the organization's responses have been very specific, pointing to particular areas where the government could intervene but has not been able to do so. Most of the services offered can be identified as:

- Social Welfare Oriented
- Education and Vocational Training
- Social Work and Rehabilitation
- Family Re-unification.
- Advocacy and Campaigns for Children Rights
- Life and Entrepreneurial Skills

i) Social Welfare Service

Almost all NGOs and street children projects begin by making sure that the children they serve get food and have a place to spend the night. As a result of this intention, most NGOs have drop-in centers and rescue centers that provide food, temporary accommodation, clothing and medical treatment. While at these centers, the children are trained to socialize together in order to encourage social cohesion and to stimulate self-confidence. The drop-in centers offer street children a brief relief from street life. The rescue centers provide overnight accommodation, recreation activities, counseling and a variety of training opportunities. Most of the street children programs that we visited began their operations by having drop-in centers, which later developed into rescue centers and finally turned into rehabilitation centers.

ii) Education and Vocational Training

Making sure all street children get primary education is one of the prime objectives of most organizations. They also provide non-formal education, particularly in the area of numeracy and literacy. Some centers also provide vocational training in various trades like carpentry, tailoring, auto-mechanics, welding and masonry.

Although sending street children to secondary school is not a priority, nevertheless, there are some organizations that invest a lot of resources in order to ensure that those street children who have completed their primary education and have passed to enter secondary education have an opportunity to do so. These different forms of education and training are sometimes offered by the NGOs themselves. In most cases, children are sponsored to attend other schools or training institutions. These institutions may be public, private or religious. Once the children have been enrolled in these institutions, their NGOs provide them with all the basic school requirements such as fees, uniforms, books and other supplies.

Non-formal education is offered to those children who cannot qualify for formal education enrollment. The non-formal programs are flexible. In most cases, they take place in the afternoon in order to allow children to continue with income-generating activities and are tailored to the needs of individual children. In most cases, many NGOs ensure that non-formal education combines literacy with business skills that can help children to run their own small-scale, income-generating projects. The vocational skills that most street NGOs strive to impart to the children include carpentry, tailoring, auto-mechanics, handicrafts, fine art, welding and other kinds of wood and iron work.

iii) Social Work and Rehabilitation

Street Children NGOs and projects on street children provide a variety of social work related services aimed at rehabilitating street children. The basic aim of all NGOs is to take children off the street. Besides benefiting from good food, basic education, literacy classes, medical care and life and work skills training, the children get vigorous counseling and moral support so that they can increase their self-esteem in order to reform their behavior. Since street life socializes children in an environment of violent gang activities and other criminal acts such as taking drugs, smoking marijuana, sniffing glue and commercial sex, children who have been living in the streets for many years require intensive counseling processes in order to transform their behavior so that they become members of the community. Besides the commercial drugs like bang, marijuana and others, glue and petrol sniffing is becoming increasingly popular among street children. Through rigorous counseling and health education, the children learn the side effects of drugs and are persuaded to quit taking them. Those who are rehabilitated and have quit taking drugs are sent to vocational training in order to acquire training in productive skills.

iv) Family Reunification

One of the primary aims of street children NGOs is to re-unite street children with their families. Our study shows that almost all NGOs believe that the best place for children to grow well is within their families. For this reason, NGOs try their level best to contact the parents of the children concerned and initiate a dialogue between children and parents in order to explore the possibility of reunification. This is not an easy process. It involves tracing the original background of the children, convincing them to re-join their families, and persuading their parents to take them back into their homes. None of the NGOs we studied took street children straight from the street to their homes, nor did they attempt to reunite the children with their families by force. The process begins at the drop-in centers, which provide a better environment than the street and also help advocates learn more about individual children and their circumstances. By staying temporarily at the center, the children begin to learn a new way of life and acquire a variety of skills that can help lead them to a self-reliant future. The drop-in centers also give the children a chance to make genuine choices that they prefer.

Sometimes these efforts fail because of the reluctance of the children themselves to go home. There are many factors that can contribute to this reluctance. In some cases, children are not willing to go back home because of the persistence of the conditions that made them run away from their homes. Some children refrain from joining their parents because of the breach of trust between them. As Shorter and Onyancha (1999) have observed in Kenya, the children feel sorry that their parents have let them down. At the same time, parents whose homes are experiencing severe poverty crises may feel uncomfortable taking in their children again. Such parents exaggerate their hardships and are less likely to exercise their responsibilities if they know that there are organizations prepared to take care of their children on their behalf (ibid). During our study, many NGOs, particularly those that are religious, complained that many families had been approaching them pleading poverty and requesting their organizations to take care of their children, particularly orphans, on their behalf. There are also cases where some parents have lied to organizations by presenting their children to them as orphans. These are some of the problems that can result from processes of institutionalizing street children and other children who are in difficult circumstances.

v) Advocacy and Campaign for Children's Rights

Most of the NGOs have gone beyond simply providing shelter, food, education and medical care. Many of them are involved in advocacy programs that focus on defending and protecting children's rights. These organizations try to create awareness concerning drug abuse, sexual exploitation, HIV/AIDs, child labor and the dangers of living in the streets. The Kuleana Center for Children's Rights of Mwanza is a good example of such NGOs. It holds workshops, seminars and international conferences on issues concerning children's rights. Kuleana has also produced a variety of books and brochures that are very easy to read. These publications make people aware of the factors that produce street children, the problems they experience and how best to assist and protect them. Besides advocacy programs, some NGOs assist children who are in trouble with law enforcement institutions like the police, courts and prisons. In 1999, the street children NGOs of Mwanza jointly managed to secure the freedom of a nine-year-old boy who had been found guilty of rape and was sentenced to life imprisonment. According to the Tanzania laws, this child was not supposed to be prosecuted in the first place. Sometimes the NGOs mobilize funds in order to pay for the costs of hiring lawyers who represent children in courts.

vi) Work Skills and Entrepreneurship

All NGOs are interested in making sure that their children are able to lead independent, self-reliant lives in the future. In order to achieve this, they strive to teach children a variety of life and work skills that can assist them in improving their welfare. Most NGOs train their children in carpentry, masonry, welding, auto-mechanics, driving, tailoring, computer skills and other vocational skills. In order to make sure that children run their own projects, some NGOs also teach business skills.

The "Child in the Sun Project" of Dar-es-Salaam provides a good example of preparing children to become self-reliant. Their center at Msowero in Kilosa provides children an opportunity to build their own homes and farms, to sell their products and handle their own money. We believe that the examples portrayed by this project ought to be followed by other organizations in Tanzania and elsewhere.

In order to ensure that children learn work and life skills by involving them in productive work (learning by doing), NGOs that have managed to get land for agriculture such as "Faraja" and "Huruma" of Iringa and Child in the Sun of Dar-es-Salaam involve their children in farming activities. The Fish for Life Ministry of Mwanza has a fishing boat and has bought fishing rods and distributed them to its children. Besides spiritual work and other activities, this NGO trains the children in fishing skills. Other NGOs would also like to get land so that the children can produce their own food while they are learning how to work in agricultural activities. However, the difficulties involved in getting land for such activities tend to hinder the implementation of such plans. Nevertheless, some NGOs operate small gardens where children produce vegetables, onions and tomatoes.

Some NGOs like Mkombozi of Moshi and Youth Cultural Information center of Dar-es-Salaam train their children to use their artistic talents like painting, singing, acting and drawing to earn a living. The street children of Mkombozi always produce postcards of their paintings. These cards are in turn sold in order to generate funds used in running the center.

In general, most NGOs try to ensure that children get practical training in various skills. The success of this varies from one NGO to another. Some NGOs are doing better than others because they have more financial resources as well as leadership that has vision and understands well what the children lack and what they need in order to change their lives.

9.4 Problems Experienced by Street Children NGOs
i) Defining the Problem of Street Children

The discussion about the services rendered by street children NGOs suggests that there are a variety of achievements so far. There is no doubt that the NGOs are doing a commendable job taking into account that the government has been silent in so far as helping street children is concerned.

Although the existence of the NGOs focusing on street children has assisted in rescuing many children who would have continued to live in a high-risk environment for many years to come, it is important to acknowledge that the services offered by the NGOs are treating the symptoms of the problem rather than the real causes of the problem of street children. Even by addressing the symptoms, the NGOs are too few to absorb all street children and are also very poor, inexperienced, lack qualified personnel and therefore, are not capable of carrying out effective comprehensive programs that can address both the symptoms of the problem and the real causes of the problem.

Our interviews with a variety of NGO leaders reveal clearly that they know that poverty, abuse, harassment, child neglect, sheer carelessness and lack of responsibility by some parents are the main factors that push children onto streets. Although they are aware of these factors, none of them seem to look for strategies that can address the real causes of street children. Many NGOs are involved in advocating for children's rights and making the communities aware about the effect of abuse and harassment and other difficulties experienced by children. Our findings reveal that none of the NGOs have designed appropriate strategies for alleviating poverty at the community or society level. No NGOs have projects aimed at making sure that the cities and towns are clean and that facilities promoting hygiene to desperate street children are available. These facilities may include public toilets, bathrooms, and safe sleeping places. We believe that NGOs must begin to address these issues if they want to solve this problem.

ii) Financial Constraints and Lack of Sustainability

Nearly all-street children NGOs that operate in Tanzania are severely plagued by financial problems and lack of sustainability. As Shorter and Onyancha (op.cit) have noted in Kenya, the same is true for Tanzania. All NGOs depend almost entirely on donor funding, and it is increasingly becoming clear now that such funding is notoriously uncertain. The NGOs are obliged to write project proposals with detailed justifications. If they succeed in getting a grant, it is usually for a specific period of time. Once the grant period expires, a new application must be submitted in order to get a new grant. The procedures for submitting grant applications are cumbersome, time-consuming, and their preparation demands a very specific kind of expertise. Unfortunately, most leaders of these NGOs lack this expertise and therefore experience difficulties in getting funded.

Since the NGOs depend on donor funding, their projects usually depend on the nature of donor politics. Donor policies change often. Sometimes donors can provide funds for infrastructure and initial capital investments, but can refrain from supporting running costs. For example, Kuleana has a lot of money but does not have any concrete plans that show how Kuleana can sustain its activities in case donor funding is not forthcoming. The way it stands now, it will be a miracle for Kuleana to survive once the donor support is not forthcoming. We believe that donor funding must focus on making street children NGOs self-reliant. Lack of sustainability is indeed threatening the future survival of many NGOs. The Bona-Baana Street Children project of Bukoba in Kagera region is a case in point. The project worked well when the funding from DANIDA and Danish Red Cross through the Kagera Health Project was forthcoming. When DANIDA stopped funding the health project in 1998, the entire Kagera Health Project and Bona-Baana Street children project collapsed, and all the street children who were undergoing rehabilitation at the Bona-Baana Centre took refuge again in the streets of Bukoba town.

iii) Coordination and Networking

As with other NGOs that deal with development issues regarding women, poverty, environment, human rights, gender, etcetera, there is a serious problem of coordination and networking among NGOs themselves and between them and government institutions. When collaboration and coordination exist, the connection has always been informal. A few organizations in Dar-es-Salaam recently formed a network of all street children NGOs that operate in the city with very limited success.

In the year 2000 a National Network of Street Children NGOs was formed and has its headquarters in Dar-es-Salaam. Whether this organization is going to be effective, it is too early to judge. In some places, like Mwanza, attempts to create a network of street children NGOs have not been successful for a variety of reasons. First and foremost is the difference in philosophies and principles that guide the activities of the different NGOs. The NGOs affiliated with religious organizations are likely to refuse to adopt policies and activities that contravene the ethics of their organization. For example, the Director of the Tanzania Children's Rescue Centre (TCRC) of Mwanza, whose organization is registered with the Christian Council of Tanzania and operates under the umbrella of the African Inland Church, told us that collaboration with Kuleana has been difficult to them because Kuleana distributed condoms to street children, held a very liberal approach to sexual issues and even taught street children about safe sex.

At the same time, some NGOs whose activities are not influenced by religious ethics, find it difficult to work with religious NGOs because they are conservative, less pragmatic, less down-to-earth and tend to put much more priority on spiritual education. There are some Christian NGOs that take in non-Christian children but continue to provide Christian education to such children. There have been cases where relatives of street children who are Moslems have ended up removing the children from street children NGOs that are run by Christians out of fear that the children were being forced into Christianity. It is also believed that founders of one street children's NGO, who were vegetarians, once decided not to provide meat meals to the street children they had recruited at their center. These differences in ideologies, philosophies and practices play a significant role in hindering collaboration between different NGOs.

Second, failure of coordination, collaboration and networking stems from the fact that priorities set by different NGOs vary greatly. Some organizations think that rehabilitation is more important than providing accommodation, food, clothing and other welfare services. Others believe that family reunification should be given more priority than training children in vocational skills and giving them education. Our study noted that some were currently putting much more emphasis on advocacy and children's rights programs than making sure that children were eating, clothing, getting medical treatment and were sleeping in facilities that promote hygiene and well being. Because of this variation, some NGOs have drop-in centers only, while others have drop-in centers as well as rescue and rehabilitation centers. Other NGOs have nothing, but just serve the children while they are in the streets. This broad variation has led to a situation where coordination and collaboration is difficult, leading to tremendous duplication of activities and efforts. Some children exploit this weakness and jump from one NGO to another for a similar service.

In every town we visited, we managed to meet some street children who had been recruited by one NGO and had finally gone back to street life. There are a variety of reasons for this. Sometimes the services offered by these NGOs are not good enough to attract children from the lure of the streets. Since some of these NGOs have very strict rules, and some of them are abusive, many children prefer freedom to life in an NGO center where the likelihood of living a prison life is great. Poor services are due to the fact that many NGOs do not have qualified, trained personnel who can handle street children well. Although some NGOs are now beginning to employ either qualified social workers or are training their own personnel, some of the staff that work in these NGOs are either primary or secondary school drop-outs who have been having difficulties finding jobs elsewhere.

Financial difficulties experienced by many NGOs lead to a situation where some of the workers are paid meager salaries or end up unpaid for several months. There are others who work on a voluntary basis. Given the severe situation of poverty that many people experience, it is indeed difficult for us to believe that such volunteers can be serious with work. In most cases, workers who are poorly paid or not paid at all tend to lack motivation to carry out their work. If opportunities for new jobs arise, such workers are likely to abandon their current positions.

We also noted that many NGOs were biased in terms of the sex of the children they served. In reality, most NGOs prefer to enroll street boys rather than girls. Even in those NGOs that take in children of both sexes, the number of street girls in their centers is negligible. We believe that NGOs must treat street boys and street girls equally, and ways must be sought to ensure that NGOs that discriminate are discouraged.

Resolving the problems that street children NGOs confront depends on the will of the NGOs themselves, their capacities and sources of funding. This also depends on the strength of the government in these issues, its political commitment and will to address them effectively. Now that the civil society is more actively involved in addressing this particular problem than the government, it is important for the state to design ways to support these activities. It is also important for the government to work closely with a variety of stakeholders to lay down appropriate guidelines for working with street children. All stakeholders who are committed to assisting street children should adopt these guidelines.

9.5 Conclusion

It is evident from this chapter that the civil society, more so than the state, is indeed playing a major role in trying to address the problem of street children in Tanzania. There is evidence that the civil society is increasingly beginning to understand that street children are victims of social, economic, political and cultural processes that are currently sweeping through sub-Saharan Africa. Street children are marginalized children who require enormous assistance, but, like the poor section of the urban population, they are the least assisted. Although the NGOs are doing commendable work, particularly in terms of social work and other related services, they are too few to absorb all street children that exist in urban Tanzania. The NGOs themselves differ from one another and have their own interests and policies. As a result, coordination and collaboration between NGOs is difficult. There are no appropriate guidelines to assist NGOs in knowing how to work with street children. This leads to a situation where what is done by one NGO might conflict with what is being advocated by another. Most NGOs experience severe funding difficulties, and those who operate well depend on donor funding. In this case, the sustainability of their activities is questionable.

Since the civil society has now shown both the will and commitment to assist street children, it is equally important for the government to support these growing initiatives in order to assist street children and their advocates. It is high time that the government provide guidelines for working with street children that can be used by a variety of stakeholders. Since most of the NGOs are providing social-work related services and are not addressing the essential causes of the problem, it is high time that NGOs also begin to look into ways of promoting social development, alleviating poverty and addressing all the processes that manufacture social inequality in a society.

Chapter 10

Recommendations and Conclusion

10.1 Introduction

It is evident from this study that the problem of street children is real, and its magnitude has reached an alarming proportion that warrants immediate attention. It is also clear from this study that we need to understand the nature of this problem within the context of the dynamics of the political economy of Tanzania, at the center of which lies the analysis of processes of social change, development and underdevelopment. These processes have been very efficient in generating the social relations of poverty in both urban and rural Tanzania. And these relations, as the findings of this study suggest, have been instrumental in creating conducive situations for the development of the street children phenomenon in Tanzania. The presence of jobless youths and children in rural and urban Tanzania is a symptom of the larger problem of poverty, which is dominant in the country. It is evident from the findings of this study that children end up leaving their families and resorting to street life when community capacity to take care of them is eroded and weakened. Kilbride *et al.* (2001) have noted in Kenya that the growing result of HIV infection in Kenya today is an increased burden and stress for the extended family, especially grandparents, who are left to care for AIDS orphans. The same is true for Tanzania. AIDS and Structural Adjustment Programs are destroying families and communities. They are also dismantling the extended family systems and network support structures that have previously existed in Tanzanian communities and acted as safety nets for children in need. There is evidence that between 1991 and 2001 there has been a small rise in the number of households headed by people who are 65 years old and above (HBS 2002).

The narratives below from two women of Ileje District illustrate in concrete terms how poverty and AIDS are destroying families, communities and survival safety nets. The first narrative is from a woman living alone with five children and the second one is from a woman who is taking care of the children of her two deceased brothers:

"I was married in 1983 and during the first four years we had two children. In 1990, my husband was forced to migrate to Zambia to work in the copper mines in order to raise money for school fees of our first child as well as for the development levy (tax), which had just been introduced in the district. Since then, I have been living alone. My husband visits us only once a year. During these few visits, I have had another three children with him. We now have five whom I have to raise alone. Although my husband sends us money, the money is indeed not enough. The agricultural land that we have is not much. Even if we had much land, we would not be able to use it all because our forces of production are poor. Two of my children have dropped out of school and are now assisting me in the farm as well as in the business of making and selling "kimpumu"(local brew). That is our life." (Lugalla and Barongo 2000)

"I am a mother of two. My husband died four years ago. My first brother died in 1993 leaving behind three children (two girls and one boy). His wife died in 1997. My second brother died in 1998 and left behind four children (two boys and two girls). His wife is now seriously ill, and there is no doubt that she is going to die too. Right now, I am taking care of my two children and the seven children belonging to my brothers. As you can see, I have a small house made of mud and thatched grass-roof. Feeding these children is a nightmare, let alone taking them to school. The four girls have now dropped out of school so that they can assist me with farm work and domestic chores. The older boys continue to go to school and assist us after school with petty trading. Sometimes they engage themselves in casual work in order to supplement our family income. The government is not paying any attention at us." (ibid.)

Although poverty and HIV/AIDS appear to be the leading factors that push children into streets, our findings reveal that there are other factors like poor parent-child communication, harassment, abuse and those that are connected with life at home. One should not forget the collapse of family structures, the disappearance of the traditional pattern of socialization and the failure of the current system of education to manufacture children who are self-reliant and self-confident. Most of the street children we interviewed stated that they were forced to abandon their families and their villages because of hardships and difficulties associated with poverty. The traditional role played by the extended family in dealing with these problems is currently in serious question. There are some children who have attempted to live with their relatives (particularly orphaned children), but have been forced to seek fortune in the streets because of poverty and hardships at home or maltreatment, and, in some cases, their relatives would not welcome them anymore. The analysis that emerges from this situation is that kinship ties and the roles played by the extended family are currently undergoing a dramatic change due to the increasing situation of poverty amidst the winds of modernization and social change.

There has been a dramatic increase in the level of poverty in the country, coupled with a high degree of unemployment, and a poor performance in the agricultural sector, which is apparently the mainstay of the economy. As we have described previously, the persistent increase in poverty levels during recent years is inevitably linked with the adoption of structural adjustment programs (SAPs) introduced by the IMF and World Bank. Since poverty lies at the heart of the problem of street children in Tanzania, improving the welfare of these children will necessarily involve a variety of strategies that are both long term and short term. These strategies will have to be policy- as well as program- and project-oriented. While on the one hand, long-term strategies must aim at ending the problem once and for all, short-term, project-oriented programs must look for ways of assisting children who are already in streets or are in the process of opting for street life. Below are those elements we think these strategies must involve.

10.2 Long Term Policy Oriented Strategies

The fact that we have identified many factors that create street children means that adopting one uniform intervention is impossible. It remains true, however, that the alleviation of poverty and eventual liberation from poverty may be the everlasting solution to this problem.

The high incidence of working or jobless children and other children in difficult circumstances is closely correlated with poverty, underdevelopment, under or unemployment, the poor incomes of parents and entire extended families living in an environment of permanent crisis. The continual pressures and hardships experienced by distressed families create a cycle of poverty. Some children drop out of school, and, like their fathers, take on low-paying jobs or casual employment at a very tender age. Daughters, like their mothers, drop out of their schools, get married at a tender age and become young mothers themselves. The children of these young mothers are likely to repeat the same pattern. Orphans suffer similar consequences. With the rapidly increasing rate of the HIV/AIDS epidemic, parents and guardians are likely to continue dying. Some orphans begin their life by loosing their parents first. Then they move to their relatives, and then their relatives die, and the children shift to new guardians. Generally, the lives of these children shift from one family to the other. Their lives end up being influenced by different paths of socialization, and this causes many problems in their cognitive and physical development. We strongly believe that, in order to improve the welfare of children and orphans, long-term policy-oriented strategies must address the larger socio-economic issues more aggressively. In brief, these large issues must include: (i) effective strategies of poverty alleviation, (ii) expansion of social services (education and health), (iii) community awareness and responsibility, and (iv) enforcing children's rights through appropriate legislation. Below, we examine the above issues of intervention in brief.

i) Poverty Alleviation Strategies

In Tanzania, poverty is rampant in both rural and urban areas. In fact, urban poverty is just an extension of rural poverty. The causes of poverty in Tanzania are multiple and fully evident. They range from poor agricultural sector performance, to unequal distribution of income among the population in rural and urban areas, unequal regional development and unequal development investment between the rural and urban areas. Cities and towns of Tanzania are purely administrative and not productive, and are, therefore, parasitic rather than generative and supportive to the rural economy. In most cases, urban investments like roads, water and electricity supplies depend on the surplus produced in the countryside. Therefore the relationship between urban and rural areas is exploitative, contradictory and full of conflicts. This urban bias has led to a situation where investments in urban areas have outpaced those in the rural areas and have ended making cities centers of attraction for rural poor.

Poverty in Tanzania is also a product of defective policies and the lack of political will and commitment to implement the necessary development measures that can boost the country's economy. Even after forty years of independence, the communication infrastructure, particularly roads, is very poor indeed. Poor communication infrastructure has had serious consequences on the performance of the economy in the country. Due to poor transport, agricultural inputs arrive late in the rural areas and become expensive, making the entire agricultural production quite unaffordable for the majority. The presence of poor roads also means that farmers have difficulties marketing their agricultural products outside, and this tends to lower their prices. What this means is that any serious policy aimed at improving the economy must focus on the improvement of roads within the country and those that link the country with the outside world.

Since the main stay of the economy is agriculture, we strongly believe that any sound economic policy must focus on more investments in this sector and in the activities that generate income for the rural and urban poor. The agricultural credit schemes that have begun in the rural areas are encouraging, but more appropriate methods are needed in order to evaluate their performance. Simply basing their success on loan repayment rates does not necessarily mean that the target groups are being reached, nor does it mean that the loans were used for the intended purpose.

There are several ways to boost the agricultural sector. The first way would be to increase the number of extension officers and community development officers. Second, the agricultural sector can improve if appropriate land policies that focus on equity are introduced. A strategy that makes sure that landless people have arable land, and that those who live on unproductive land are given arable land can be very helpful in reducing the situation of poverty and enhancing equality in the rural areas. Attempts must be made to make sure that the majority of people have easy access to the major means of production, particularly land.

Many people, particularly youths and children, are flooding cities and towns because of the advantages of economies of scale that these towns offer. Water, electricity, business and marketing infrastructure services are relatively abundant in these places. The rural areas of Tanzania do not have electricity, and very few villages have a reliable supply of water. It is even surprising that several transmission lines of electricity throughout the country serve one city to the other while passing over of several unlit villages. We believe that sound economic policies must note the fact that rural electrification is one of the most important supportive measures in alleviating poverty in the rural areas. This can enhance the development of light industries and informal sector economic operations and can also initiate the establishment of small-scale agricultural products' processing industries. Such a development can have many advantages positively impacting the condition of the rural poor. Some of these advantages are: The potential for increasing the value of agricultural products and the provision of rural employment in order to eradicate rural-urban migration. This can also reduce the developmental gap between rural and urban areas. Through these policies, it is also possible to raise family incomes and therefore promote the welfare of several families and, more specifically, the welfare of young children. The provision of safe water means that the people can be protected from a variety of water-borne diseases. There is no doubt that this will promote social development in the entire countryside. If the economy grows up as a result of these investments, then the likelihood that family incomes will grow is greater. If incomes of the poor increase, there is a better hope that parents will be able to afford paying for both the health and education of their children and might probably refrain from exposing their children to employment opportunities that are dangerous.

While improvement of social life in the rural areas is taking place, strategies to reduce urban poverty must also be on the agenda of politics and development. Shorter and Onyancha (1999), in their study of street children in Nairobi, Kenya have shown the importance of promoting the urban informal sector which has the potential of absorbing the majority of the unemployed poor. This has to go hand in hand with the improvement of such civic and social services infrastructure such as roads, housing, power, sanitation, health and education institutes. These services must be easily accessible and affordable to the majority poor.

ii) Expanding Education and Health Infrastructure
(a) Access to Formal Education

Street children, like any other children, have the right to education. Education is important to these vulnerable children because it can develop their potential and improve their socio-economic conditions. The government, NGOs and parents must make an effort to ensure that all children who are of school eligible age go to school. Once they have enrolled, these efforts must ensure that the children continue with their education. Arrangements must be made to make sure that pregnant girls are not expelled from school, but continue with education after delivery. A study of children in need of special protection measures in Tanzania by UNICEF (1999) has argued that it is not sufficient to discuss the need to give educational and skills opportunities without addressing the sexuality of young people. This requires sex education at both school and community levels. But sex education needs to be fully integrated into the whole system of education. If health education is treated as a separate topic, it both arouses hostility and fails to be integrated into social and personal behavior patterns. Reproductive health must be taught to girls as well as to boys. Both must learn a variety of life skills. Girls need to learn how to negotiate sex and to say "no" to risky sexual encounters.

Efforts must be focused on finding solutions for the underlying problems causing school dropouts. As the UNICEF study argues, these efforts must address the following key issues:

- poverty, where the family cannot afford to pay the school fees and other expenses such as uniforms, school equipment and schoolbooks
- poverty and other circumstances, where children and adolescents are forced to work in order to survive instead of attending school

135

- child-headed households, where children and adolescents, especially girls have responsibility for younger children, and therefore cannot attend school.
- children having negative experiences at school because of violence, abuse and severe punishments.

The bottom line here is that long-term policy strategies must ensure that all children have easy access to education and are retained and integrated into the formal education system. It is evident from our study that most of the jobless/working street children interviewed in Dar-es-Salaam are school drop-outs or never went to school at all. We have also shown that primary education is too theoretical and irrelevant to local conditions, problems and needs. By the time children graduate from these schools, they are indeed unskilled, are too young to begin an independent life, and hence resort to street life. The children resort to street life because they have nowhere to go after graduating from primary education. The other reason is due to the hardships they experience in their homes and school environment. It is also clear from our study that there are very few secondary schools compared to the thousands of children who graduate from primary schools. Also, there are very few schools for the disabled or post primary vocational education institutions. In reality, even if the children who finished primary education were interested in going for further education (vocational or secondary), the schools for them to join, even if they had money, do not exist. It is our opinion that, in order to deal with this situation, the following interventions may be deemed appropriate:

First, expansion of secondary education by increasing the number of schools in the country in general, but particularly in rural areas, is necessary. This should be done simultaneously with an expansion of the capacity of the existing schools. One way of minimizing the cost of this exercise is to open more secondary day schools. Second, many vocational or post-primary technical education facilities where primary school graduates can learn technical/productive skills such as masonry, carpentry, iron works, tailoring, pottery and other life skills must be opened.

A study in Ileje District has concluded that if planners of development policies and strategies learn from the voices of the poor themselves, communities are willing to invest their labor and effort in building such schools or centers (Lugalla and Barongo 2000). The government can then enhance these processes by supporting local initiatives. This can be done via the provision of equipment, technical advice, and experts (teachers for example). Since opening technical training centers is an expensive exercise, the easiest possibility is to look for ways to provide support to private workshops that operate in rural areas, so that they can train youths in different skills for a nominal fee (Lugalla and Barongo 2000).

In order to reduce drop-out rates and the rates at which children fail to join schools because of poverty (particularly orphans), arrangements should be made so that they can be exempted from paying school fees and other contributions. Children lacking proper school uniforms should not be expelled from school. We strongly believe that such regulations are discriminative, tend to antagonize the parents and the school system, and end up creating more ignorant children than literate ones. All development policies must be cognizant of the fact that poor parents need assistance and not condemnations or prosecutions in the court system. Evidence from several studies quoted in the previous chapters reveal that parents complained about the school environment and about the way teachers treated their children. The street children we interviewed confirmed these complaints. Poor facilities at school and lack of incentives to both teachers and students tend to demoralize them and encourage some to run away from school. Unnecessary brutality and abusive punishments (i.e. corporal punishment) exacerbate the development of negative attitudes toward schooling among many students. It is therefore important to look for ways to improve the school infrastructure so that the atmosphere and environment is supportive to learning processes and cognitive development. The curriculum should be relevant to local conditions and needs. Lugalla and Barongo (2000) recorded the following narrative from a street boy in Ileje District, Tanzania:

"I was eight when I began to assist my mother in selling locally made bread (*sambusa*). By then, I was in the second grade. The business was lucrative and I began having money of my own. Sometimes I had to skip school in order to do this job, particularly during the weekly open markets. My performance at school was not good, and was punished frequently by my teachers for both poor performance and absenteeism. At eleven I dropped out of the school and continued with this job. I am now 16. Some of my friends who continued with school and graduated are also doing the same thing. What is the difference between them and I? What is the use of staying in school?"

Such attitudes toward schooling should be viewed in the context of the general perception about the irrelevance of primary education to children's daily lives in Tanzania. Parents as well as community leaders who took part in some of our discussions described the difficulties they have in convincing their children of the importance of school in the prevailing situation where the schools are not well-equipped and have fewer teachers who are often demoralized by an appalling school

137

environment in which the curriculum is irrelevant and the chances for further education are remote.

We believe that it is important to make sure that the education the children get can assists them first in finding solutions to basic problems that they confront in their local areas. What transpires in school, in terms of teaching practical skills, must reflect the local conditions of life. The orientation of the school curriculum toward more practical contents and the life environment of the students can help to ensure that skills children learn are relevant to their daily lies. Such a curriculum can improve the welfare of children and reduce their constant drift to towns. This is a challenge to the entire system of education in Tanzania. Knowing that Tanzania is different both geographically and in terms of natural resources and having a uniform school curriculum for the entire country is a contradiction of the highest order. Education can produce good results if there is constant communication between teachers, parents and children. As we are writing this conclusion, there is good news that the government of Tanzania has decided to abolish school fees in public primary schools. This is a good start, but more needs to be done. Abolishing other contributions that schools require parents to pay should follow this.

b) Access to Non-Formal Education

It is also important to initiate non-formal education so that we can impart knowledge to school drop-outs, working children and girls who cannot attend school for the entire day. Alternative support to formal schooling has worked well in some countries, and, we believe, if perceived well, can also work well in Tanzania. This should target those who cannot be re-integrated into the formal education system. Besides imparting skills, this education should focus on learning tools like reading, writing numerals, and different learning domains (e.g. knowledge, norms, society values, productive skills and life skills). Since street children and orphans are not a homogeneous group, the non-formal education, due to its freedom and flexibility in designing programs, can be of great assistance to these vulnerable children. Flexibility makes it possible to adjust the learning and teaching programs and to tailor a training course specifically to the background and needs of each child. It is also very important to use a child-centered teaching approach for street children since they have different backgrounds and many of them lack basic skills. Since street children are busy fending for themselves, it is very likely that education provided on a part-time basis might be most favored.

In brief, in order to make sure that street children and orphans have access to education and productive training, programs must focus on basic education, vocational training, and entrepreneurial training. All these can be achieved by both formal and non-formal systems of education.

c) Health

Children can grow well and become active participants of their own liberation if they are healthy. Most children who are in difficult circumstances are continually exposed to an environment that puts their health at risk. They have difficulty accessing clean water, a good diet and medical treatment. Our study noted that street children have difficulties maintaining hygiene. Public sanitation facilities like toilets and water are hard to find in most urban areas in Tanzania. One easy way to assist these children would be for the town fathers to make sure that at least clean public toilets and water kiosks are available and easily accessible. It is important to make sure that children are well cared for in terms of basic needs and that those from poor families have easy access to health care. Since most children in the streets are in their adolescent years, counseling on general hygiene and reproductive health can be very helpful in protecting children's health.

In brief, delivery systems of social services must reach out to families so that they can strengthen the capacity of both the family and the community in order to provide a conducive environment for children and a head start for a healthy life. The children or, in general, Tanzanian youth must be given the opportunity to learn life skills that can protect them from a variety of deadly epidemics like HIV/AIDS. Findings from several studies show that in Tanzania, children, adolescents and youth become sexually active at a very tender age (Kapiga *et al.* 1992, Leshabari 1988, Seha *et al.* 1994, Lwihula *et al.* 1996, Lwihula 1997). These findings are supported by national data from the National AIDS Control Program which has shown a cumulative AIDS case rate of 281 per 100,000 females aged 20-24 years and 140 per 100,000 males of a similar age (NACP 1994). The HIV prevalence rates among teenage male blood donors (15-19 years) increased from 0% in 1987 to 3.3% in 1990, while for girls of the same age, it increased from 0% to 7.5 % during the same time period (Kaaya *et al.* 1997). A study in 2000 showed that out of the boys who were sexually active, only 15% had sex with one partner. The remaining 85% engaged in multiple sexual relationships. About 11% had ever used condoms while 89% engaged in unprotected sex. Eight percent of those involved in multiple sex relationships stated that they had used a condom once, but it was the first and last time they had done so (*Sunday Observer* December 5, 2002). This alarming information confirms that the situation is almost out of control. These statistics suggest that Tanzania needs to adopt pragmatic, down-to-earth policies in order to protect this young population. The present trend of hesitating to introduce sex education is counterproductive. Equally counterproductive are policies against advocating condom use in schools or using condoms as an exhibit for incriminating a suspected dealer in commercial sex (prostitute), as the story below from *The Guardian* newspaper of Tanzania (December 31, 2002) tells.

"Arusha prostitutes say that police are partly responsible for fueling the spread of HIV virus because they discourage use of condoms, the rubber protective gear said to reduce chances of infection if properly used during sex. Women prostitutes who talked to journalists who were attending a workshop in Arusha recently, said police would arrest and send them to court, if they found condoms which they hid in their handbags. They say police take the condom as evidence that the suspect is a prostitute. To avoid this, some of the prostitutes have dropped the habit of carrying condoms when they go about selling sex. As a result, they gamble their lives away, hoping to find condoms in guest rooms hired by their male partners. Meanwhile, there are allegations that are some individuals in rural areas who use one condom more than once. Similarly one condom can be used by more than one person."

iii) Community Awareness and Responsibility

Studies in Kenya, Brazil and elsewhere have shown that, in spite of the good intentions and extensive efforts accompanying the numerous programs for helping street children, the attitude of the general public toward them remains largely negative (Shorter and Onyancha 1999, Diversi 1999, Lugalla and Mbwambo 1999). Our study has revealed that most people have mixed feelings about street children. We believe that the welfare of children in difficult circumstances can improve if the general public is also involved in solving these problems. The attitude of people towards these children has to change. Without public sympathy and support, the rights of children and their dignity will not be respected. It is important to develop awareness of child abuse and neglect in communities and families. Enhancing community awareness should not only be theoretical (i.e. through advocacy alone); rather, poor families and their children, together with other members of the society, must be involved in decision making processes that affect their lives. Peoples' sense that they are worthy can facilitate effective interventions.

There is a strong belief in rural and urban Tanzania that childcare is a woman's main responsibility. It is also evident from our findings that poor women use their children to supplement their meager incomes. In a poor country like Tanzania, the need to fulfill the double role played by women (production and reproduction) puts an enormous amount of strain on poor women. Assistance with childcare can provide a great relief to these women. Community-run and oriented day care centers can play an important role in reducing the burden of childcare performed by women. It is also important to make sure that fathers know that it is their responsibility to take care of children. The present Maternal and Child Health Program tends to enhance gender inequality and stereotyping since it only targets women and children. Husbands and male children also need to learn about childcare and child health. Men must be involved in issues related to family planning. This can be accomplished via health education strategies that are comprehensive and realistic.

Development strategies must focus on mobilizing people to manage their own affairs. It is important for development planners to know that people have always been creative. They are not ignorant of their problems and needs, but what they need are supportive policies and strategies and an enabling environment. What they need is assistance and advice in what they are doing. If development planners acknowledge this fact, they can raise both awareness and development consciousness and can mobilize their communities to participate effectively in transforming their own environment and solving the pertinent problems that confront them. We need to involve families and communities in all programs that focus on the rehabilitation of street children. As Shorter and Onyancha (1999) have observed in Kenya, families are largely absent from the process by which street children are rehabilitated. Sometimes, in order to empower these communities, the local governments need to establish a system where part of the taxes paid at local levels remain at local levels (i.e. village governments) so that the funds can be used to promote development and social welfare in villages. The people must control their money and must experience the importance of paying taxes. This can happen if taxes are used to promote local development. Taxes paid by the local communities and retained at the community level can also be used to support families that are in difficult circumstances and need help. Such families include the one represented by a female widow from Ileje below.

"I am a mother of two. My husband died four years ago. My first brother died in 1993 leaving behind three children (two girls and one boy). His wife died in 1997. My second brother died in 1998 and left behind four children (two boys and two girls). His wife is now seriously ill, and there is no doubt that she is going to die. Right now, I am taking care of my two children and the seven children belonging to my brothers. As you can see, I have a small house made of mud and thatched grass roof. Feeding these children is a nightmare, let alone taking them to school. The four girls have now dropped out of school so that they can assist me with farm and domestic work. The older boys continue to go to school and assist us after schoolwork with petty trading. Sometimes they engage themselves in causal work in order to supplement our income. The government is not paying any attention to us"(Lugalla and Barongo, 2000).

Similarly, an orphaned girl from the same area narrated her ordeal in the following way:

"Our mother died five years ago. We are three and I am the only girl in the family. Since the death of our mother, we have been living with our father but we hardly see him during the day. He is always out. He leaves the house early in the morning and comes back very late at night, sometimes drunk. Sometimes he spends some of the nights with his new girlfriend. In case of an emergency, we always get help from our neighbors"(ibid.).

If such families get access to funds available at the community level, they will be able to use them for initiating small-scale income generating projects. These funds can lead to self-reliance and economic independence.

iv) Children's Rights Through Appropriate Legislation

Family poverty, abuse, harassment and parental irresponsibility and carelessness contribute simultaneously to the creation of street children and enhance the problems experienced by most children in difficult circumstances. As members of the family, children are abused and beaten by their parents. As students, they are harassed and beaten by their teachers, and when they opt for street life, they also risk being beaten by adults and being sexually abused and molested by street gangs. Therefore, work with children in need of special protection measures must proceed from a rights, rather than welfare, perspective. Although Tanzania is a signatory of the United Nations Convention on the Right of the Child and has some laws with the objective of protecting children, children in general, and particularly those in difficult circumstances, continue to suffer from discrimination, abuse, harassment and hardship. This is largely due to both lack of appropriate legislation and a failure on the part of the government to enforce the existing laws. Our study has shown that the definition of a child in Tanzania is contextual and varies from one law to another, depending on the purpose of that law. The Child Development Policy looks at children as a homogeneous group. There is no attempt to understand that children differ in terms of their social economic backgrounds, physical appearance, abilities and talents. Having a blanket policy for all children in Tanzania is counter-productive. There is a need to revise all children's laws so that they can protect them well. All those laws that create room for child abuse have to be repealed. For example, the 1978 Education Act that keeps maintaining the use of corporal punishment in schools is likely to enhance processes that encourage child abuse. All policies that consider the parents' habit of beating their children as socially and culturally appropriate are likely to enhance severe child abuse. There is a need to have policies that advocate the plight of children as innocent victims of the circumstances surrounding them. Hostile and punitive attitudes toward street children must be replaced by more need-based child-centered initiatives.

A study in Ileje noted that some street children and orphans did not know what was considered abuse and what was not. Even when such children are severely abused, they do not know where to turn for assistance. In general, what we are trying to argue here is that most children are ignorant of their rights. In order to make sure that children know their rights and how to defend them, arrangements must be made to make sure that children are aware of their rights and that they can distinguish between an ordinary warning, harassment and abuse. This can be achieved by using the existing education facilities, i.e. primary schools. There is a need to introduce courses that teach children or make them aware of their rights and how to protect themselves. For example, it is important to teach children about the role of the police force in society. It is also important to teach the police, so that they know that their role in society is to protect members of the society and not to harass them. Right now, the relationship between the police and street children is full of fear and mistrust. The fact that most children fear the police is a reflection of how the police force is divorcing itself from members of society. Children are members of families. Domestic violence and parents abusing each other have negative consequences not only for couples themselves, but also for the welfare of children. Domestic violence is rampant in Tanzanian families, and existing policies and laws are not only inadequate, but tend to be silent toward these issues. Coupled with gender inequality, women suffer greatly as a result. And since they are the prime caretakers of the domestic sphere of life, including the welfare of children, their suffering affects immensely the welfare of children. The story narrated below by a woman who left her husband is concrete evidence of this situation.

"My father is the one who is taking care of us. Our mother died in 1999. Although I am married with three children, I left my husband because he was physically abusing me. I wanted to stop producing children but he wanted more children. When I suggested family planning to him he terribly bit me. When I attempted to refuse having sex with him, he also bit me. It is because of these reasons that I decided to return back to my parents. But when this happened, my husband went to the village government and accused my father for taking me (his wife) away from him. The village government ordered me to go back to him since I had left him without informing them, or else my father will have to pay him a cow. Although I have not yet returned to my husband, I am now worried because my father is now very sick. We are very poor, and my sibling and I have never been to school. Since I might be going back to my husband, I decided to go to a family planning clinic where I got an injection. I am not sure whether it will work. Let me tell you one thing. In this area, it is wastage of time to report the abusive acts of the husband to the village government. The village government is dominated by men who believe strongly that once you are married, you are supposed to obey what the husband says and demands"(Lugalla and Barongo, 2000).

The analysis resulting from the above experience shows that it is important to design policies and laws that address domestic violence and all forms of spousal abuse and that protect vulnerable members of the family like women. Formulating policies and enacting laws aimed at protecting children and their mothers can remain useless if the establishment of an effective mechanism of enforcing them is not there. This can succeed only if there is true and effective cooperation between the general public, the police, the judiciary and other relevant organizations. We believe that these can be mutually supportive if they understand well the nature of the legislation and its objective. At the same time, it is important to enhance legal education, knowledge and awareness, so that those who are always victims can understand their situation and be able to fight for and defend their rights. The work that is currently carried out by the Tanzania Women Media Association (TAMWA), Tanzania Association of Women Lawyers (TAWLA) and Tanzania Gender Networking Program (TGNP) is a good start in the right direction.

In addition to knowing that street children are at high risk of maltreatment by adults, the government of Tanzania has never developed a welfare policy aimed at protecting them. Most of the laws in Tanzania that focus on protecting children tend to lump together street children, orphans and other children without taking into account the fact that street children are, in fact, a disadvantaged group of children who suffer a double jeopardy, first as children, and secondly as street children.

Street children in urban Tanzania continue to rely on charity. As Shorter and Onyancha have noted, these organizations have formulated and developed their programs based on their own views of childhood and adolescense. Some religious organizations have shaped their programs on the basis of religious notions of salvation through work and prayer rather than by scientific knowledge of child and adolescent development (Shorter and Onyancha 1999). Other NGOs have gone to the extent of distributing condoms and teaching safe sex to street children, an issue that has caused a severe uproar among residents in some parts of Tanzania. Whether that is the direction of socializing children that Tanzania would like to pursue remains to be seen. It is not in our interest to advocate the establishment of NGOs to deal with street children matters, but we must make sure that the processes of raising people's awareness on children's rights is part and parcel of the processes aimed at making people aware of these problems. Once this is clear, it is possible for the people to assume the responsibility of protecting children and defending their rights. Policies must make sure that community members are facilitators of children's priority needs. The rural poor can and must be part of the solution rather than a liability.

10.3 Short-Term Program/Project Oriented Strategies

While on the one hand, the long-term, policy-oriented strategies are aimed at solving the problem once and for all, on the other hand, the short-term, project-oriented ones are aimed at assisting children in difficult circumstances who need immediate help. Although we would indeed like to discourage the development of institutions aimed at accommodating children and 'rehabilitating' them, we believe, however, that some programs need to be established in order to solve the immediate needs of these children. The programs can focus on the following key issues: productive skill development, promotion of small-scale income generating cooperatives and foster parenting. We examine in brief each of these below.

i) Productive Skills Development Programs

These children lack marketable skills to obtain gainful employment. Even those who have some kind of regular work can barely sustain life. If street children are to be prepared for work in the formal and informal sectors, they certainly need training in skills that can offer them gainful employment or at least give them the power to bargain in the labor market. Although with Structural Adjustment Policies of downsizing, it is indeed difficult to secure waged employment in Tanzania, we believe that skills training is an important strategy to ensure that child and youth labor is not exploited. If these children and youths have productive skills, it is possible for them to live a self-reliant life.

ii) Promotion of Small-Scale Income Generating Cooperatives

One way to alleviate the terrible conditions of street work and reduce the risk of labor exploitation is to organize working children into small cooperatives. Although this approach is difficult to implement, there is mounting evidence that street children live and work in groups in order to protect themselves. Further research studies are

145

needed to understand street children group dynamics and how one could harness them to create cooperatives run and led by the children. If children learn how to work together, they can also defend their interests and rights together or in groups. This means that cooperative activities can enhance the process of empowerment for working youths and children.

Productive cooperatives are an important step in the right direction because they can be part and parcel of income-generating processes and can therefore improve the welfare of children. By working in cooperatives, children can learn how to share ideas, lead groups and exchange experiences. If street children are provided with small-scale credit schemes in order to establish income-generating projects that not only give them income but also train them in specific skills, it is very likely that most children will be able to live a decent, independent life in the future. Surviving in the streets alone makes them very vulnerable. They need to be helped to work together while washing cars, barking for transport vehicles, shining shoes and also while working as prostitutes. As has been demonstrated in this study, street children are usually good at organizing themselves, and development planners need to learn from them in order to be able to provide advice and guidance.

iii) Foster Parenting

Our study has noted the rapidly increasing rate of orphaned children due to HIV/AIDS in Tanzania and how this is associated with the increase in the number of street children. While programs on health education are ongoing, in order to reduce the speed of the epidemic, we believe that it is important now to establish pragmatic ways of assisting orphaned children. We strongly recommend the following strategies in order to assist the orphaned children. One is to support the existing networks of the extended family so that relatives or members of the family prepared to take care of the children who have lost their parents can be able to do that comfortably. The second possibility is to identify foster parents prepared to live with orphans. Once these parents are identified, arrangements should be made so that they can be assisted in terms of food, education and health care costs, and probably other general costs, too. Putting orphans in orphanages can make children suffer psychologically as they are isolated from ordinary social life. If orphans live with the extended family/relative or foster parents, they can be socialized in an ordinary family life and, therefore, enjoy life like any other children.

10.4 Conclusion

Eliminating the problems facing street children and other children in difficult circumstances will take several years to accomplish. Improving their welfare is also a gradual process that will involve a variety of stakeholders, effective networking and coordination among different institutions. Since many, if not most, of the problems experienced by children in difficult circumstances arise from the exploitation, harassment, or negative attitudes by adults, there is a crying need to educate the public so that they can treat these children as children and not as objects of exploitation.

Eliminating poverty requires comprehensive long-term policies that focus on improving the quality of life by focusing on basic needs like food, shelter, clean water, employment, health, education and security. Development policies must acknowledge the fact that development in general is a process and not a product or state. Benefits of development must be available to all, and development must encompass social improvement and not merely be a matter of capital works. As far as Tanzania is concerned, development must be seen in terms of social progress, economic growth in the agricultural sector, increased equity and health, and the improved welfare of all people. If this happens, the end result will be the improvement of the welfare of children in difficult circumstances such as street children and orphans.

Urban poverty in sub-Saharan Africa in general and Tanzania in particular is a manifestation of rural poverty. Urban problems cannot be adequately addressed without adequately addressing the factors associated with rural underdevelopment and growing rural poverty. Experiences from other countries, such as China, Indonesia, and Vietnam, suggest that it is possible to improve rural urban inequality by adopting specific strategies of development. These include employing new technical and organizational knowledge, expanding access to markets for agricultural produce and harnessing new biological, chemical and mechanical inputs (World Development Report 1999/2000).

This can be achieved if a country does the following. First, establishes a network support system that creates and enhances trust between the urban and rural producers. There must be a backward and forward linkage between the urban and rural sectors. Urban areas must not totally depend on surplus produced from the countryside, but must also support rural development by being generative and productive. They must produce things/commodities that are in need in the rural areas or can lead to a revolutionary transformation of the agricultural sector. The rural farmers of Tanzania suffer enormously from the lack of appropriate information that can change their way of thinking, producing and reproducing. They also lack good infrastructure, transportation and easy access to small-scale credit facilities. Due to this, production continues to be predominantly of the subsistence type and of small-scale in nature.

Secondly, an efficient economy requires an efficient infrastructure. The communication and road network and other forces of telecommunication systems that link rural producers and service providers between urban and rural areas in Tanzania are inherently underdeveloped and are very poor indeed. Only 12 percent of Tanzania's roads are in good condition and passable throughout the year. The remaining 88 percent are so poor that they impose excess damage to vehicles leading to a tremendous rise in operating costs and accidents. Improved communication is vital for a developing nation like Tanzania; not only will it link the rural and urban areas, but also can bring the country closer to the global economy. Good infrastructure can facilitate an easy spread of agricultural/industrial research and extension services to the rural economy.

There is no way Tanzania can avoid the sweeping winds of globalization and modernization. But globalization without control is very dangerous for young nations like Tanzania. It is therefore important for Tanzania to design solid policies that can control globalization and mitigate the negative social and economic consequences of the globalization process. Besides controlling the process, it is important for Tanzania to exploit the advantages that can be achieved from it. The need to attract foreign investments that can revolutionize the economy and make it self-sustaining is imperative. However, creating a conducive environment for investments involves creating credibility in the eyes of foreign investors. Unfortunately, of late, Tanzania has been viewed as one of the world's most corrupt countries (World Development Report 1999/2001).

All the interventions suggested in this study can work well if they involve the community in general, but particularly families. Experience shows that interventions managed from the top down have not worked well in many countries. At the same time, there is ample evidence that interventions can become effective if they are client driven and customized to the needs of the local people themselves. Besides alleviating family poverty, a strong emphasis should be placed on education for children and on skills training and job creation for parents and adults. Political initiative, commitment and will are necessary to make sure that comprehensive intervention dealing with causes rather than symptoms are implemented effectively.

In order to enhance our understanding of the nature of street children in sub-Saharan Africa, more research in this area is needed. As Rakesh and Kudrati (1994) have argued, it is important to:

- Research the specific situation of children in communities, especially the relationship between adults and children, paying particular attention to issues of violence, abuse and the specific needs of children orphaned by AIDS
- Increase and expand basic services to poor communities, especially in health, education, water and sanitation
- Identify and strengthen community approaches of caring for children.

148

- Conduct an assessment of the situation of children for all interventions, projects, and programs prior to planning, in evaluating the effects/benefits to children, and during the evaluation of the intervention. Special efforts should be made to elicit and incorporate the views of children in this process.

We strongly believe that if Tanzania and other countries in sub-Saharan Africa implement the suggestions offered in this study, the problem of street children can become a closed chapter. This can only be achieved successfully if the political will and commitment of the government is there and if it is accompanied by people's willingness and commitment to resolve the problem. It can be done if all of us play our part.

149

Aptekar, L. and Stocklin, D. "Growing Up in Particularly Difficult Circumstances: A Cross-Cultural Perspective." *Handbook of Cross-Cultural Psychology v. 2 Basic Processes and Human Development.* J.W. Berry, P.R. Dasen, and T.S. Swaraswathi, eds. Needham Heights, Massachusetts: Allyn and Bacon, 1997.

Aptekar, L., et al. "Street Children in Nairobi: Gender Differences in Mental Health." *Homeless and Working Youth Around the World: Exploring Developmental Issues: New Directions for Child and Adolescent Development # 85.* Marcela Raffaelli and Reed W. Larson, eds. San Francisco: Jossey-Bass, 1999. 35-46.

Aptekar, L., Cathey, P.J., Ciano, L.M., and Giardino, G. "Street Children of Nairobi, Kenya." *African Insight* 20.3 (1995): 250-259.

Bagachwa, M.S.D. and Maliyamkono, T.A.L. *The Second Economy in Tanzania.* Athens, Ohio: Ohio U P, 1990.

Bassuk, E. and Rubin, L. "Homeless Children: A Neglected Population." *American Journal of Orthopsychiatry* 57.2 (1987): 279-286.

Blanc, S.C. *Urban Children in Distress: Global Predicaments and Innovative Strategies.* Langhorne, PA: Gordon & Breach, 1994.

Brannen, J., ed. *Mixing methods: Qualitative and Quantitative Research.*: Aldreshot: Avebury, 1992.

Chachage, S.L.C. "Urban Capitalism in Tanzania: An Example of Arusha Town." Diss. University of Dar-es-Salaam, 1983.

Chalamila, G. "Experience of the Dar-es-Salaam Youth Health Clinic." *International Conference on Street Children and Street Children's Health.* Dar-es-Salaam: 19-21 April 2000.

Cooksey, B. and Mmuya, M. "Education, Health, and Water: A Baseline Service Delivery Survey for Rural Tanzania." *TADREG Working Paper Series No. 5.* Dar-es-Salaam: TADREG, 1997.

Cooksey, B. Malekela, G. and Lugalla, J.L.P. "Parent's Attitude Towards Education in Rural Tanzania." *TADREG Research Report No. 5.* Dar-es-Salaam: TADREG, 1993.

Coulson, A. *Tanzania: A Political Economy.* New York: Clarendon Press, 1982.

DANIDA. "Project Evaluation Report." *Primary Education Report (PEP).* Dar-es-Salaam: DANIDA, 1996.

Dietz, P. and Coburn, J. *To Whom do They Belong? Runaway, Homeless, and Other Youth in High-Risk Situations in 1990s.* Washington DC: National Network of Runaway and Youth Services, 1991.

Diversi, M., Filho, N.M., and Morelli, M. "Daily Reality on Streets of Campinas Brazil." *Homeless and Working Youth Around the World: Exploring Developmental Issues: New Directions for Child and Adolescent Development # 85.* Marcela Raffaelli and Reed W. Larson, eds. San Francisco: Jossey-Bass, 1999. 19-34.

Ferreira, M. Luisa and Griffin, Charles. "Tanzania Human Resources Development Survey Final Report." Population and Human Resources, Eastern Africa Department. Washington, DC: World Bank, 1995.

Governo do Estado do Ceara/Secretaria de Acao Social. "Perfil do Menino e Menina de Rua de Fortaleza." Fortaleza. Mimeo. *Urban Children in Distress: Global Predicaments and Innovative Strategies.* S.C. Blanc, ed. Langhorne, PA: Gordon & Breach, 1994.

IBGE/UNICEF. Criancas e Adolescentes-Indicadores Sociai, vol.1. Rio de Janeiro:IBGE/UNICEF. *Urban Children in Distress: Global Predicaments and Innovative Strategies.* S.C. Blanc, ed. Langhorne, PA: Gordon & Breach, 1994.

Ishumi, A.G.M. *The Urban Jobless in Eastern Africa: A Study of the Unemployed Population in the Growing Urban Centres, with Special Reference to Tanzania.* Uppsalla: Scandinavian Institute of African Studies, 1984.

Kaaya, S.F., Kilonzo, G.P., Semboja, A. and Matowo, A. "Prevalence of Substance Abuse Among Secondary School Students in Dar-es-Salaam." *Tanzania Medical Journal* 7.1 (1992): 21-24.

Kaaya, S.F., Leshabari, M.T., and Mbwambo, J.K. "Risk Behaviors and Vulnerability to HIV Infection Among Tanzanian Youth." *Journal of Health and Population in Developing Countries* 1.2 (1997): 51-60.

Kapiga, S.H. and Lugalla, J.L.P. "Sexual Behavior Patterns and Condom Use in Tanzania: Results from the 1996 Demographic and Health Survey." *AIDS Care* 14.4 (2002): 455-469.

Kapiga, S.H., Hunter, D.J., and Nachtigal, G. "Reproductive Knowledge and Contraceptive Awareness and Practice among Secondary School Pupils in Bagamoyo and Dar-es-Salaam, Tanzania." *Central African Journal of Medicine* 38.9 (1992): 375-380.

Kilbride, P., Suda, C., and Njeru, E. *Street Children in Kenya: Voices of Children in Search of a Childhood.* Westport, Connecticut: Bergin & Garvey, 2000.

Kilonzo, G.P., Mbwambo, J.K., Kazaura, M.R., Kisesa, A.F. and Chachage, C.L.S. "Pilot Study on School Health Promotion in Dar-es-Salaam." Collaborative Research with Universities of Bergen and Zimbabwe: A Preliminary Report." 1995.

Kipokola, J.P. "Tanzania Country Report." *Through Structural Adjustment to Transformation in Sub-Saharan Africa.* H.M. Mlawa and R.H. Green, eds. Dar-es-Salaam: Dar-es-Salaam U P (1996) Ltd., 1998.

Knaul, F. "Counting the Street Children of Bogota: Defined Away, Missing or Out of Sight." *Working Paper Series no. 95-07.* Cambridge, MA: Harvard Center for Population and Development Studies, 1995.

Knaul, F. "Young Workers, Street Life and Gender: The Effect of Education and Work Experience on Earnings in Colombia." Diss. Harvard University, 1995.

Kondoro, J.W.A., Lugalla, J.L.P. and Majani, B.B.K. *"Options for Improved Urban Pollution Control and Management: A Case Study of the Dar-es-Salaam Msimbazi Valley"* A Research Report submitted to International Development Research Council, Ottawa, Canada, 1996

Kulaba, S.M. "The Provision and Management of Housing in Urban Areas: A Case Study of Dar-es-Salaam." *Seminar on Living in the Cities.* Dar-es-Salaam: Goethe Institute, 1987.

Kuleana. *The State of Education in Tanzania: Crisis and Opportunity.* Mwanza, Tanzania: Kuleana, 1999.

Leshabari, M.T. "Factors Influencing School Adolescent Fertility Behavior in Dar-es-Salaam, Tanzania." Dissertation John Hopkins University, 1988.

Leshabari, M.T., Kaaya, S.F., Nguma, J.K., and Kapiga, S.H. "Household responses to HIV/AIDS in Mbeya Region, Tanzania." Dar-es-Salaam: Institute of Public Health, University of Dar-es-Salaam, 1996.

Lesthaeghe, R. *Reproduction and Social Organization in Sub-Saharan Africa.* Berkeley: University of California P, 1989.

Le Roux, J. "Street Children in South Africa: Findings from Interviews on the Background of Street Children in Pretoria, South Africa." *Adolescence* 32 (1996): 423-431.

LeVine, R. A. *Child Care and Culture: Lessons from Africa.* Cambridge: Cambridge University P, 1994.

Lipumba N.H.I., et al. *Economic Stabilization Policies in Tanzania: Workshop Papers.* Dar-es-Salaam: Economics Department, University of Dar-es-Salaam: Economic Research Bureau, 1984.

Lugalla, J.L.P., et al. "The Social and Cultural Contexts of HIV/AIDS Transmission in the Kagera Region, Tanzania." *Journal of Asian and African Studies* 34.4 (1999): 378-402.

Lugalla, J.L.P. *Adjustment and Poverty in Tanzania.* Hamburg/Muenster, Germany: Lit Verlag, 1995.

Lugalla, J.L.P. *Crisis Urbanization and Urban Poverty in Tanzania: A Study of Urban Poverty and Survival Politics.* Lanham, Maryland: University Press of America, 1995.

Lugalla, J.L.P and Mbwambo, J.K. "Street Children and Street Life in Urban Tanzania: The Culture of Survival and its Implication on Children's Health." *International Journal of Urban and Regional Research* 23.2 (1999): 229-34.

Lugalla, J.L.P. "Development, Change, and Poverty in the Informal Sector During the Era of Structural Adjustments in Tanzania." *Canadian Journal of African Studies* 31.3 (1997): 424-451.

Lugalla, J.L.P. and Barongo, V.I. "Profiles of Rural-Based and Orphaned Children in Ileje District, Tanzania: A Research Report." Dar-es-Salaam: UNICEF, 2000.

Lugalla, J.L.P. and Kibassa, C.G., eds. *Poverty, AIDS and Street Children in East Africa.* Lewiston, New York: Edwin Mellen Press, 2002.

Lugalla, J.L.P. "The Impact of Structural Adjustments on Women and Children's Health in Tanzania." *Review of African Political Economy 63* (1995):43-53.

Lwihula, G.K. "Baseline survey on Factors which Inhibit or Facilitate Behavior Change among Out-of-School Youth (10-18 Years) with Regard to HIV/AIDS in Two Rural Districts, Musoma and Kisarawe, Tanzania." Unpublished research report. Dar-es-Salaam: Institute of Public Health, Muhimbili University College of Health Sciences, 1997.

Lwihula, G.K., Nyamuryekung'e, K., and Hammelmann, C. "Baseline Survey of Sexual and Reproductive Health Knowledge, Perceptions and Behavior among School Youth in Kinondoni District." Dar-es-Salaam: African Medical Research Foundation (AMREF), 1996.

Mabala, R. and Kamazima, S.R. *The Girl Child in Tanzania: Today's Girl, Tomorrow's Woman: A Research Report.* Dar-es-Salaam: UNICEF, 1995.

Manundu, M. "Structural Adjustment Programs in Emerging Democracy: The Case of Kenya." *Conference on the Rule of Law and Democracy in the 1990s and Beyond.* Nairobi: Law Society of Kenya, 1991.

Mbatia, J. "Drug Trafficking." *Drug Abuse Prevention: A Handbook for Educators in Tanzania.* J. Mbatia and G.P. Kilonzo, eds. Dar-es-Salaam: Mental Health Association of Tanzania and Health Education Unit, Ministry of Health, 1996.

Mbunda, L. "Does the Law in Tanzania Protect Street Children: An Appraisal of the Legal Regime Governing Street Children." *Poverty, AIDS and Street Children in East Africa.* J.L.P Lugalla and C.G. Kibassa, eds. Lewiston, New York: Edwin Mellen Press, 2002. 161-175.

Miles, M.B. and Huberman, A.M. *Qualitative Data Analysis: A Sourcebook of New Methods.* Beverly Hills: Sage Publications, 1984.

Ministry of Education and Culture (MOEC). "Basic Statistics in Education, 1993-1997." *National Data.* Dar-es-Salaam: The United Republic of Tanzania, 1998.

Mlawa, H.M. and Green, R.H., eds. *Through Structural Adjustment to Transformation in Sub-Saharan Africa.* Dar-es-Salaam: Dar-es-Salaam U P (1996) Ltd., 1998.

MNMMR, IBASE, & NEV/USP. Vidas em Risco:Assassinatos de Criancas e Adolescentes no Brasil. Rio de Janeiro: MNMMR.*Urban Children in Distress: Global Predicaments and Innovative Strategies.* S.C. Blanc, ed. Langhorne, PA: Gordon & Breach, 1994.

Mpangile, G.S., Leshabari, M.T., and Kihwele, D.J. "Factors Associated with Induced Abortion in Public Hospitals in Dar-es-Salaam, Tanzania." *Family Planning Association of Tanzania (UMATI)*. Dar-es-Salaam: November, 1993.

Mutuku, M. and Mutiso, R. "Kenya: The Urban Threat for Women and Children." *Urban Children in Distress: Global Predicaments and Innovative Strategies.* S.C. Blanc, ed. Langhorne, PA: Gordon & Breach, 1994. 217-258.

Narayan-Parker, Deepa. *Voices of the Poor: Poverty and Social Capital in Tanzania.* Washington D.C.: The World Bank, 1997.

National AIDS Control Program (NACP). *National AIDS Control Programme HIV/AIDS/STD Surveillance Report No. 8.* Dar-es-Salaam: Ministry of Health, United Republic of Tanzania, 1994.

National Bureau of Statistics and Oxford Policy Management, Ltd., UK, *Household Budget Survey (HBS)* Final Report, Dar-es-Salaam, Tanzania, May 2002.

Olenja, J. and Kimani, V.N. "Poverty, Street Life, and Prostitution: The Dynamics of Child Prostitution in Kisumu, Kenya." *Poverty, AIDS and Street Children in East Africa.* J.L.P Lugalla and C.G. Kibassa., eds. Lewiston, New York: Edwin Mellen Press, 2002. 47-68.

Oliveira, C. de F.G.(1989). Se Essa Rua Fosse Minha-Um Estudo sobre a Trajetoria e Vivencia dos Meninos de Rua do Recife. Recife:UNICEF. *Urban Children in Distress: Global Predicaments and Innovative Strategies.* S.C. Blanc, ed. Langhorne, PA: Gordon & Breach, 1994.

Onyango, P., et al. "Research on Street Children in Kenya." Unpublished report. 1990.

Outwater, A. *"The Socioeconomic Impact of AIDS on Women in Tanzania." Women's Experiences with HIV/AIDS: An International Perspective.* Lynellyn D. Long and E. Maxine Ankrah, eds. New York: Columbia University Press, 1996.

Oxfam International. "Debt Relief for Tanzania: An Opportunity for a Better Future." Oxfam International Position Paper, Oxfam, 1998.

Patel, S. "Street Children, Hotel Boys and Children of Pavement Dwellers and Construction Workers in Bombay--How They Meet Their Daily Needs." *Environment and Urbanization* 2.2 (1990): 9-26.

Porio, E. "Becoming and Being a Street Child: Survival Contexts, Strategies, and Interventions." Florence: The Urban Child Project, UNICEF International Child Development Center, 1990.

155

Rajani, R. and Kudrati, M. "The Varieties of Sexual Experience of the Street Children Of Mwanza, Tanzania." *Learning about Sexuality: A Practical Beginning.* S. Zeidenstein and K. Moore, Eds. New York: Population Council, International Women's Health Coalition, 1996: 301-322.

Rizzini, I., et al. "Brazil: A New Concept of Childhood." *Urban Children in Distress: Global Predicaments and Innovative Strategies.* UNICEF. Langhorne, P.A.: Gordon and Breach, 1994.

Schoepf, B.G. "AIDS Gender and Sexuality During Africa's Economic Crisis." *African Feminism: The Politics of Survival in Sub-Saharan Africa.* G. Mikell, Ed. Philadelphia: University of Pennsylvania P, 1997.

Schoepf, B.G. "Health, Gender Relations, and Poverty in the AIDS Era." *Courtyards, Markets, and City Streets: Urban Women in Africa.* K. Sheldon, ed. Boulder, Colorado: West View Press, 1996.

Schoepf, B.G. "Political Economy, Sex, and Cultural Logics: A View from Zaire." *African Urban Quarterly 6.1-2* (1991): 94-106.

Seha, A.M., Klepp, K.I., and Ndeki, S.S. "Scale Liability and Construct Validity: A Pilot Study Among Primary School Children in Northern Tanzania." *AIDS Education and Prevention* 6: (1994): 524-534.

Shorter, A. and Onyancha, E. *Street Children in Africa: A Nairobi Case Study.* Nairobi, Kenya: Pauline's Publications Africa, 1999.

Sibthorpe, B., Drinkwater, J., Gardner, K., and Bammer, G. "Drug Use, Binge Drinking and Attempted Suicide among Homeless and Potentially Homeless Youth." *Australian and New Zealand Journal of Psychiatry* 29 (1995): 248-256.

Smollar, J. "Homeless Youth in the United States: Description and Developmental Issues." *Homeless and Working Youth Around the World: Exploring Developmental Issues: New Directions for Child and Adolescent Development # 85.* Marcela Raffaelli and Reed W. Larson, eds. San Francisco: Jossey-Bass, 1999. 47-58.

Sumra, S. "An Analysis of National and Regional Enrollment Trends in Primary Education in Tanzania." Unpublished report. Dar-es-Salaam: UNICEF, 1995.

UNICEF. *Complementary Basic Education in Tanzania (COBET).* Dar-Es-Salaam: UNICEF, 1998.

UNICEF. *Children in Need of Special Protection Measures: A Tanzanian Study.*

Dar-es-Salaam: UNICEF, 1999.

UNICEF. *Women and Children in Tanzania: A Situation Analysis.* Dar-es-Salaam: The Government of the United Republic of Tanzania: UNICEF, 1990.

UNICEF. "Executive Summary of Basic Education in Tanzania: Briefing Note for Ms. Fay Chung, Head, Education Section and UNICEF." New York: 1997.

UNICEF. *The State of the World's Children.* Oxford: Oxford University P for UNICEF, 1989.

UNICEF. *The State of the World's Children.* Oxford: Oxford University P for UNICEF, 1993.

United Nations Association of the USA, United Nations Association of Minnesota. *A Child's Right, A Safe and Secure World: The United Nations Convention on the Right of the Child.* New York: United Nations Association, USA, 1991.

United Republic of Tanzania. *Report of the Presidential Commission of Inquiry into Land Matters.* Dar-es-Salaam: Ministry of Lands, Housing, and Urban Development, Government of the United Republic of Tanzania, 1994.

United Republic of Tanzania. *Child Development Policy.* Dar-es-Salaam: Ministry of Community Development, Women Affairs and Children, Government of the United Republic of Tanzania, 1996.

United Republic of Tanzania. *The 1978 National Education Act.*

United Republic of Tanzania. *The Affiliation Ordinance Cap No. 378.*

Verma, S. "Socialization for Survival: Developing Issues Among Working Street Children in India." *Homeless and Working Youth Around the World: Exploring Developmental Issues: New Directions for Child and Adolescent Development # 85.* Marcela Raffaelli and Reed W. Larson, Eds. San Francisco: Jossey-Bass, 1999. 5-18.

Weisner, T.S., et al., Eds. *African Families and the Crisis of Social Change.* Westport, Connecticut: Bergin & Garvey, 1997.

World Bank. "Tanzania Agriculture Sector Memorandum." *Vol. II: Main Report.* Washington, DC: Agriculture and Environment Operations Divisions, East Africa Department, Africa Region, 1994.

World Bank. *"Entering the 21st Century: World Development Report 1999/2000"* Oxford University Press, 2000.

About the Authors

Dr. Joe L.P.Lugalla is a Tanzanian currently working as an associate professor at the University of New Hampshire in United States of America. He holds a Bachelor of Arts degree and a Master of Arts degree from the University of Dar-es-Salaam, Tanzania and a Doctor of Philosophy degree in Social Sciences from the University of Bremen, Federal Republic of Germany. He has published/edited books and numerous articles in International Journals in the areas of poverty, urbanization, international development, globalization, international health and HIV/AIDS.

Dr. Colleta G. Kibassa is a Tanzanian Consultant Pediatrician who, until March 2003, was a National Coordinator of Integrated Management of Childhood Illnesses in the Ministry of Health in Tanzania. She holds medical degrees from Odessa Medical Institute in Ukraine and the University of Dar-es-Salaam. She is currently the UNICEF'S Project Officer of Health and Nutrition in Harare, Zimbabwe. Her main areas of interest are in Reproductive and Child Health, and she has published extensively in this area.

Summary

Research studies on the health conditions of children living in difficult circumstances in sub-Saharan Africa are rare or just beginning. Although there are a number of studies that have focused on street children, few of them have paid attention to the hardships and violence these children endure in harsh urban environments and how this affects their health. In this book, Lugalla and Kibassa examine the dynamics of urban life and street children's health in the era of globalization and structural adjustments in Tanzania. They discuss the factors that push children out of their homes, how the children survive in streets, the hardships and violence they endure and how this affects their health. They argue that the impact of the legacy of colonial policies and some post-colonial development policies, the negative consequences of uncontrolled processes of globalization, the impact of structural adjustments and the HIV/AIDS epidemic are simultaneously intensifying the situation of poverty in Tanzania. These processes are not only destroying families and communities that have for many years acted as safety nets for children in need, but are also manufacturing poor, helpless and powerless children, most of whom resort to street life. While in the streets, children experience a harsh life characterized by hardships and violence. This life puts the health of children in jeopardy and exposes them to HIV infection. The authors suggest that any attempt to end this problem must begin with the adoption of comprehensive policies that address the above issues adequately.

Afrikanische Studien

Gabriele Altheimer; Veit Dietrich Hopf;
Bernhard Weimer (Hg.)
Botswana
Vom Land der Betschuanen zum Frontstaat.
Wirtschaft, Gesellschaft, Kultur
Mit Botswana begegnet uns eine scheinbar
friedliche und wohlhabende Insel inmitten der
Krisenregion des südlichen Afrika. Afrikanische
und europäische AutorInnen zeichnen in 28
Beiträgen dem deutschsprachigen Leser hier erst-
malig ein ausführliches Bild von der Geschichte,
Wirtschaft und Kultur dieses Landes, das viele
Beobachter als Wirtschaftswunder und demokra-
tisches „Musterland" in Afrika einschätzen. In
Gesprächen, Fallstudien und literarischen Texten
entfaltet sich lesebuchartig das vielgestaltige und
widersprüchliche Leben in Botswana.
Bd. 1, 2. Aufl., 1997, 350 S., 19,90 €, br.,
ISBN 3-88660-511-6

Stefan Brüne; Joachim Betz;
Winrich Kühne (eds.)
**Africa and Europe: Relations of Two
Continents in Transition**
The end of the East-West conflict, the
establishment of the Single European Market
and the ongoing economic decline of many
African countries have considerably changed the
framework for European-African relations. The
European Community would be able to assert a
stronger influence on African governments today
if the major member states shared common policy
goals and coordinated their policies. However,
European economic and strategic interest in
Africa is rapidly diminishing, exemplified by
the lowering of Europe's diplomatic presence in
Africa and the uncertain future of institutional
links such as the CFA Franc Zone. Rising
"Afropessimism" could also be seen as an
opportunity freeing European-African relations
from the pursuit of narrow self-interest and
outdated cultural ties and paving the way for
the harmonization and coordination of African
policies within Europe. The essays in this book
focus on the interests of individual European
states (France, Germany, Great Britain, Italy,
Portugal) in maintaining close relations with
Africa and in harmonizing their approaches
within the European Union as a whole.
Bd. 2, 1994, 272 S., 19,90 €, br., ISBN 3-89473-714-x

Michael Bollig; Doris Bünnagel (Hg.)
Der zentralafrikanische Regenwald
Ökologie, Geschichte, Gesellschaft, Wirt-
schaft

Nur wenige tausend Kilometer von den europäischen Metropolen entfernt existieren im Herzen
Afrikas noch riesige zusammenhängende Re-
genwälder. In der Diskussion um die weltweite
Regenwaldvernichtung spricht bei uns kaum
jemand von den bedrohten Wäldern Zentralafri-
kas. Geringe Bevölkerungsdichte und schwierige
politische Strukturen haben die großflächige
Erschließung dieser einzigartigen Ökosysteme
bisher verhindert. Dabei träumte bereits der
Afrikaforscher Henry Morton Stanley von einer
wirtschaftlichen Ausbeutung des Kongobeckens,
als er in den 70er Jahren des letzten Jahrhunderts
den Kongolauf kartografierte.
In Westafrika ist heute der Ausverkauf der ver-
kehrsgünstig küstennah gelegenen Tropenwälder
weitgehend abgeschlossen – die Waldflächen der
Elfenbeinküste oder Nigerias sind auf weniger
als 10 Prozent ihrer ursprünglichen Ausdehnung
geschrumpft. Deshalb beginnen nun europäische,
vor allem deutsche Holzkonzerne, nach den un-
zugänglichen zentralafrikanischen Tropenwäldern
zu greifen. Das zentralafrikanische Land Zaïre,
fünfmal so groß wie Frankreich, ist heute noch
zu 80 Prozent mit tropischen Wäldern bedeckt.
Wie lange noch?
Bd. 3, 1993, 248 S., 17,90 €, br., ISBN 3-89473-577-5

Werner Biermann
Wachuurizi Na Halasa
Händler und Handelskapital in der
wirtschaftlichen Entwicklung Ostafrikas
(900 bis 1890)
Bd. 5, 1993, 328 S., 30,90 €, br., ISBN 3-89473-712-3

Ulrich van der Heyden;
Achim von Oppen (Hg.)
**Tanzania: Koloniale Vergangenheit und
neuer Aufbruch**
Die Frage nach den Chancen und Grenzen eines
neuen Aufbruchs stellt sich angesichts der "Wen-
de" in Tanzania, wie auch in anderen Staaten
Afrikas, heute ganz neu. Sie bildet den Ausgangs-
punkt für zusammengefaßten Rückblicks
auf 100 Jahre kolonialer und nachkolonialer
Vergangenheit dieses ostafrikanischen Landes.
Die einzelnen, thematisch gegliederten Beiträge
beschäftigen sich dabei auch mit der besonderen
Rolle, die Deutsche in Tanzania immer wieder
gespielt haben: als Entdeckungsreisende, Kauf-
leute, Missionare, Soldaten, Kolonialbeamte,
Pflanzer, Wissenschaftler und Entwicklungsex-
perten. Andererseits kamen auch immer wieder
Menschen aus Tanzania nach Deutschland, um
hier zu arbeiten, zu lernen und zu leben. Die Geschichte dieser wechselseitigen, wenn auch meist
ungleichen Verknüpfung wirft erneut die Frage

LIT Verlag Münster – Hamburg – Berlin – London
Grevener Str./Fresnostr. 2 48159 Münster
Tel.: 0251 – 23 50 91 – Fax: 0251 – 23 19 72
e-Mail: vertrieb@lit-verlag.de – http://www.lit-verlag.de

nach der Verantwortung für die Zukunft auf.
Bd. 7, 1996, 160 S., 15,90 €, br., ISBN 3-8258-2146-3

Werner Biermann
**Tanganyika Railways – Carrier of
Colonialism**
An Account of Economic Indicators and
Social Fragments
Bd. 9, 1996, 150 S., 19,90 €, br., ISBN 3-8258-2524-8

E. Adriaan B. van Rouveroy van Nieuwaal;
Werner Zips (eds.)
**Sovereignty, Legitimacy, and Power in
West African Societies**
Perspectives from Legal Anthropology
Africa has been given persistently the negative
image of the lost continent: political turmoil,
economic failures, hunger, disease, irresponsible
and irrational warlords and corrupt regimes.
Such a bias calls for a critique. The authors seek
to analyse power divisions and struggles over
sovereignty and legitimacy in African societies
from a historical point of view. Possibilities for
peaceful social relations are taken as much into
account as internal frictions between state and
"traditional authorities". In a striking difference
to the legitimacy claims of single-rooted states,
political legitimacy in many African states derives
from two sources: the imposed European colonial
states and the pre-colonial African polities. State
and traditional authorities (systems of chieftaincy)
depend on each other's contributions in striving
towards the goals they both desire to achieve
in the fields of development, stable *democratic*
governance and human rights.
"Indigenous" institutions are not necessarily
inferior to state institutions. The opposite might
be true in view of the capacity of the traditional
institutions not just to decide internal disputes,
but actually to solve them and thus contribute
to social cohesion. Such a perspective is highly
relevant for a variety of concrete social relations
of which gender relations are one important
aspect.
Bd. 10, 1998, 264 S., 19,90 €, br., ISBN 3-8258-3036-5

Beat Sottas; Thomas Hammer;
Lilo Roost Vischer; Anne Mayor (Hrsg./éd.)
**Werkschau Afrikastudien – Le forum
suisse des africanistes**
Die Werkschau versucht eine Standortbestim-
mung des gegenwärtigen Schaffens einer jüngeren
Generation schweizerischer Forscherinnen und
Forscher, welche sich mit Afrika beschäftigen.
Der innere Bezug zwischen den verschiedenen
Aufsätzen wird in den Ausführungen zur Entste-
hung und zur Bedeutung des Forums dargelegt.
Einige Überlegungen zur Wissenschaftspolitik

zeigen Entwicklungsperspektiven auf. Die insge-
samt 34 Beiträge aus Geschichte, Ethnologie und
Archäologie, zu den Geschlechterbeziehungen, zu
Gesundheitsfragen, zu Umwelt und Raumplanung,
zur Afrikalinguistik sowie zum Themenkreis Li-
teratur und aktuelles Theaterschaffen sind sieben
thematischen Schwerpunkten zugeordnet. Wäh-
rend einige der AutorInnen mit ihren Beiträgen
nur einen flüchtigen Blick auf Ideenskizzen oder
work in progress gewähren, gelingt es anderen,
innovative Impulse zu vermitteln, ja neue Themen
aufzugreifen und mögliche Annäherungen zu
skizzieren.
Bd. 11, 1997, 392 S., 24,90 €, br., ISBN 3-8258-3506-5

Hans van den Breemer;
Bernhard Venema (eds.)
**Towards Negotiated Co-management of
Natural Resources in Africa**
Within the field of management of natural
resources, this book focuses on the various
approaches of policy formulation and
implementation. The question central to this
book is how to co-operate with people, the
various categories of residents as well as non-
residents, in the rural areas: in a top-down, a
participatory or a contractual (co-management)
way. On the basis of a comparative analysis of 12
case studies in the book, these three approaches
are thoroughly discussed and their internal and
external constraints examined.
The book starts with an editorial chapter,
discussing the recent administrative and political
developments in Africa as well as the new
opportunities, which they offer for policies in
the field of environment, and development.
The question is brought up whether the recent
processes of decentralization, democratization,
and empowerment of local organizations have
indeed created new opportunities or that they
have only superficially changed the political
culture of the countries concerned.
In the concluding chapter of the book, the
approaches are contrasted to each other as
logical models, each with its own potentiality
and limitations. Conclusions are formulated
why the top down approach must result in
improvization to escape from failure, and why
the participatory approach risks to end up into a
mixed balance. Special attention is given to the
conditions and the prospects for the contractual
or co-management approach, which has been
introduced into Africa only recently. Under
certain conditions, this approach seems rather
promising.
Bd. 12, 1999, 368 S., 25,90 €, br., ISBN 3-8258-3948-6

LIT Verlag Münster – Hamburg – Berlin – London
Grevener Str./Fresnostr. 2 48159 Münster
Tel.: 0251 – 23 50 91 – Fax: 0251 – 23 19 72
e-Mail: vertrieb@lit-verlag.de – http://www.lit-verlag.de

Lilo Roost Vischer; Anne Mayor;
Dag Henrichsen (Hrsg./éd.)
Brücken und Grenzen – Passages et
frontières
Werkschau Afrikastudien 2 – Le forum suisse
des africanistes 2
Afrikaforschung in der Schweiz: Dieser Band
ist der zweite in der Reihe "Le forum suisse
des africanistes" der Schweizerischen Afrika-
Gesellschaft. Er umfasst 30 Beiträge, haupt-
sächlich von jüngeren Forscherinnen und For-
schern unterschiedlicher Disziplinen, zu den
Themenbereichen "Forschungsbeziehungen und
Umsetzung", "Umwelt, Ressourcen und Wirt-
schaftsräume", "Lokales Wissen, Aufbau und
Entwicklung", "Besiedlung, Technologie und
Migration", "Grenzerfahrungen und Versöhnung",
"Missionsgeschichte", "Sprache und Repräsentati-
on" sowie "Stimmen, Texte und Erinnerung".
Recherches africaines en Suisse: Ce volume est le
second de la série "Le forum suisse des africanistes" de la Societé suisse d'études africaines. Il
contient 30 articles, pour l'essentiel écrits par des
jeunes chercheurs de differentes disciplines, sur
les domaines "Politique de la recherche, contextes
et rencontres", "Milieux, ressources et espaces
économiques", "Savoirs locaux, reconstruction et
développement", "Peuplements, technologies et
environnements", "Délimitations et réintegrations
sociales", "Histoire des missions", "Dénomina-
tions et langage" ainsi que "Textes et voix pour
mémoires".
Bd. 13, 1999, 480 S., 25,90 €, br., ISBN 3-8258-4398-x

Fred Krüger; Georgia Rakelmann;
Petra Schierholz (Hg.)
Botswana – Alltagswelten im Umbruch
Facettes of a Changing Society
Die Gesellschaft Botswanas verändert sich rapide.
Dieses Buch greift damit verbundene aktuelle
gesellschaftliche Prozesse auf und zeigt, wie fa-
cettenreich und von welchen Konflikten begleitet
sich der rasche soziale Wandel vollzieht.
Autorinnen und Autoren aus Botswana und
Deutschland schlagen einen großen Bogen von
dem sich verändernden Alltagsleben in Dör-
fern und Städten über die Entwicklung neuer
kultureller und sprachlicher Identitäten hin zu
den wachsenden Umweltproblemen im fragilen
Ökosystem der Kalahari. Ihre dokumentarischen,
erzählerischen und wissenschaftlichen Beiträge vermitteln schlaglichtartig einen tiefen und
spannenden Einblick in gegenwärtige Lebenssi-
tuationen in diesem ungewöhnlichen afrikanischen
Land.
Bd. 14, 2000, 224 S., 15,90 €, br., ISBN 3-8258-4671-7

Deutsch-Madagassische Gesellschaft e. V.
(Hg.)
Madagascar: Perspectives de
Développement
Croissance de la Population et Croissance
Economique contre Sauvegarde de la Nature
Auch wenn der Freundschaftsvertrag zwischen
Deutschland und Madagaskar schon vor über
einhundert Jahren unterzeichnet worden ist, ge-
hört Madagaskar nicht zu den Ländern, die im
Mittelpunkt der deutschen Entwicklungspolitik
stehen. Die Hinwendung Deutschlands zu den
osteuropäischen Ländern nach 1999 hat diese
Tendenz noch verstärkt.
Zu Unrecht; denn Madagaskar ist ein kleiner
Kontinent für sich. Nirgendwo auf der Welt gibt
es so viele Tiere und Pflanzen, die endemisch
sind, das heißt, die nur auf Madagaskar und nicht
woanders vorkommen.
Wirtschaftswachstum und Bevölkerungsexplosion
haben jedoch dazu geführt, daß ein großer Teil
dieser einzigartigen Fauna und Flora bereits aus-
gerottet ist oder vom Aussterben bedroht ist.
Im August 1998 trafen zum ersten Mal deutsche
und madagassische Wissenschaftler in Madagaskar zusammen, um gemeinsam Lösungsansätze
zur Abwendung dieser ökologischen Katastro-
phe zu erarbeiten. Das Symposium unter dem
Thema "Madagaskar: Entwicklungsperspektiven – Bevölkerungs- und Wirtschaftswachstum
contra Erhalt der natürlichen Umwelt" fand in
Mahajanga an der Nordwestküste Madagaskars
statt.
Die teilnehmenden Wissenschaftler – Biologen,
Soziologen, Wirtschaftswissenschaftler, Mediziner,
Geologen u. a. – erörterten das Thema aus dem
Blickwinkel ihrer jeweiligen Disziplinen.
Bd. 15, 2000, 344 S., 20,90 €, br., ISBN 3-8258-4807-8

Joe L. P. Lugalla; Colleta G. Kibassa
Urban Life and Street Children's Health
Children's Accounts of Urban Hardships and
Violence in Tanzania
The authors examine the dynamics of urban
life and street children's health in the era
of globalization and structural adjustments
in Tanzania. They discuss the factors that
push children out of their homes, how the
children survive in streets, the hardships and
violence they endure and how this affects
their health. They argue that the impact of
the legacy of colonial policies and some post-
colonial development policies, the negative
consequences of uncontrolled process of
globalization, the impact of structural adjustments
and the HIV/AIDS epidemic are simultaneously
intensifying the situation of poverty in Tanzania.
These processes are not only destroying families

LIT Verlag Münster – Hamburg – Berlin – London
Grevener Str./Fresnostr. 2 48159 Münster
Tel.: 0251 – 23 50 91 – Fax: 0251 – 23 19 72
e-Mail: vertrieb@lit-verlag.de – http://www.lit-verlag.de

and communities that have for many years acted as safety nets for children in need, but are also manufacturing poor, helpless and powerless children most of whom resort to street life.
Bd. 16, Frühj. 2003, ca. 168 S., ca. 20,90 €, br., ISBN 3-8258-6690-4

Christoph Haferburg; Jürgen Oßenbrügge (Eds.)
Ambiguous Restructurings of Post-Apartheid Cape Town
The Spatial Form of Socio-Political Change
Bd. 17, Frühj. 2003, ca. 200 S., ca. 20,90 €, br., ISBN 3-8258-6699-8

Manfred O. Hinz; Thomas Gatter (Eds.)
Local Government and Traditional Authority in Southern and Western Africa
The Problem of Legitimacy Global Responsibility as a Local Agenda – Towards the Legitimisation of Modern Self-Government and Traditional Authority. Proceedings of a conference held 19 to 21 April, 2002, at Bremen University
Bd. 18, Frühj. 2003, ca. 256 S., ca. 25,90 €, br., ISBN 3-8258-6782-x

Konfrontation und Kooperation im Vorderen Orient
herausgegeben von Prof. Dr. Ferhad Ibrahim
(Freie Universität Berlin)

Ferhad Ibrahim; Abraham Ashkenasi (Hg.)
Der Friedensprozeß im Nahen Osten – Eine Revision
Der Ende 1991 mit der Madrider Friedenskonferenz begonnene Nahostfriedensprozeß, in dessen Zentrum die Lösung des israelisch-palästinensischen Konfliktes steht, markiert einen fundamentalen Wendepunkt im Nahostkonflikt. Die seit Jahrzehnten virulente Frage nach der Anerkennung und der politischen Gestaltung des Selbstbestimmungsrechts der Palästinenser ist irreversibel und mit vorrangiger Priorität auf die Agenda der am Friedensprozeß beteiligten Staaten gerückt. Dennoch scheint dieser Prozeß seit den israelischen Wahlen im Mai 1996 in eine Sackgasse geraten zu sein. Es wird deutlich, daß der israelisch-palästinensische Konflikt, der in seinem Kern aus dem Anspruch zweier Völker auf dasselbe Land hervorging, sich gegenwärtig verstärkt in der Auseinandersetzung diversifizierter und heterogener Gesellschaften präsentiert. Die Beiträge des vorliegenden Buches fokussieren den Friedensprozeß der letzten sechs Jahre unter

Berücksichtigung zentraler Entwicklungen der israelischen und der palästinensischen Gesellschaft. Die Analysen zeigen Hemmnisse und Perspektiven des Friedensprozesses auf. Ausblicke auf die syrische und jordanische Positionierung verdeutlichen die regionale Bedeutung und Komplexität der israelisch-palästinensischen Annäherung.
Bd. 1, 1997, 448 S., 20,90 €, br., ISBN 3-8258-3341-0

Ferhad Ibrahim
Konfessionalismus und Politik in der arabischen Welt
Die Schiiten im Irak
Der Konfessionalismus wird im Nahen Osten von den Anhängern des arabischen Nationalismus, aber auch von den Islamisten als Atavismus und Partikularismus abgelehnt. Dennoch basieren die politischen Systeme in dieser Region in der Regel auf konfessionellen, ethnischen oder kommunalistischen Bindungen und Loyalitäten. In dieser Studie wird der Versuch unternommen, den offensichtlichen Widerspruch zwischen den erwähnten Bindungen und Loyalitäten und dem ideologischen panarabischen oder islamistischen Anspruch offenzulegen. Dabei wird in der vorliegenden Studie der Begriff "politischer Konfessionalismus" als Analyseinstrument herausgearbeitet, um am Beispiel des Irak die Gründe für die politische Desintegration und Instabilität transparent zu machen.
Bd. 2, 1997, 392 S., 35,90 €, gb., ISBN 3-8258-3350-x

Stefan Braun
Duell zweier Freunde
Die USA und Israel bei der Friedenssuche im Nahen Osten
Die USA und Israel – das klingt nach enger wirtschaftlicher und militärischer Zusammenarbeit, nach einer ungewöhnlich ausgeprägten Freundschaft zwischen zwei Ländern. Auf den ersten Blick stimmt diese Wahrnehmung. Die USA standen vor fünfzig Jahren am gegründeten Staat in jedweder Situation zur Seite. Dahinter verbarg sich die Überzeugung der Amerikaner, daß sie die Regierungen in Israel nur dann zu notwendigen Kompromissen gegenüber ihren Nachbarn bewegen könnten, wenn die Israelis sich durch die US-Hilfe stark und unverletzlich fühlten. Dieses Prinzip des Gebens und Nehmens hat sich jedoch in den letzten zwanzig Jahren ins Gegenteil verkehrt: Die Stärke Israels ist heute ein, wenn nicht das Haupthindernis für die Verwirklichung eines Friedens mit den Palästinensern. Die vorliegende Untersuchung zeigt, wie es zu der engen Bindung zwischen beiden Staaten kam, wie sehr dabei Außen- und Innenpolitik miteinander verflochten sind und wie sich die Friedenssuche im Nahen Osten nach dem Abkommen von Camp David

LIT Verlag Münster – Hamburg – Berlin – London
Grevener Str./Fresnostr. 2 48159 Münster
Tel.: 0251 – 23 50 91 – Fax: 0251 – 23 19 72
e-Mail: vertrieb@lit-verlag.de – http://www.lit-verlag.de

1978 zu einem spannenden Duell zweier Freunde entwickeln konnte.

Bd. 3, 1999, 472 S., 30,90 €, br., ISBN 3-8258-4014-x

Ferhad Ibrahim; Gülistan Gürbey (eds.)
The Kurdish Conflict in Turkey
Obstacles and Chances for Peace and Democracy
The kidnapping and condemnation of the PKK Leader Abdullah Ocalan represent a turning point in the development of the Kurdish problem in the Middle East. Although the Turkish state achieved a strategic victory, the Kurdish conflict is yet to be politically solved. The question whether the Turkish state elite will be willing in this new context to change its repressive policy against the Kurds and assume a new political orientation remains open.
In the current volume social scientists from different disciplines analyse the various dimensions and aspects of the Kurdish conflict. At the core of the interest are the controversy on the political implementation of violence, the relevance of the international law for the conflict, the regional and foreign relations of the PKK, and the chances and obstacles of a peaceful democratic conflict resolution. CONTENTS: Hamit Bozarslan, *"Why the armed Struggle?" Understanding the Violence in Kurdistan of Turkey;* Michael Gunter, *The Kurdish Question and International Law;* Gülistan Gürbey, *Peaceful Settlement of Turkey's Kurdish Conflict through Autonomy;* Amr Hamzawy, *Contemporary Arab Academic and Journalistic Perceptions of the Kurdish Problem;* Ferhad Ibrahim, *The "Foreign Policy" of the PKK: Regional Allies and Enemies;* Robert Olson, *Turkey's Relations with Syria since Gulf War: The Kurdish Question and the Water Problem;* Baskin Oran, *Linguistic Minority Rights in Turkey, the Kurds, and Globalization;* Norman Peach, *International Law and the Kurdish Struggle for Freedom;* Heidi Wedel; *Migration and Displacement – Kurdish Migrants in Instanbul in the 1990s*

Bd. 4, 2000, 216 S., 17,90 €, br., ISBN 3-8258-4744-6

Curd-Torsten Weick
Die schwierige Balance
Kontinuitäten und Brüche deutscher Türkeipolitik
Die deutsche Türkeipolitik verlief bis zum Ende der siebziger Jahre auf ruhigen Bahnen, geriet jedoch zu Beginn der achtziger Jahre in zunehmendem Maße in Turbulenzen. Vor dem Hintergrund neuartiger und zudem höchst komplexer innen- und außenpolitischer Problemstellungen sah sich die Bundesregierung nunmehr zu einer schwierigen Balance zwischen real- und moralpolitischen Interessenkalkülen genötigt. In diesem Kontext unternimmt die Studie den Versuch, Kontinuitäten und Brüche deutscher Türkeipolitik darzustellen und zu bewerten.

Bd. 5, 2001, 408 S., 35,90 €, br., ISBN 3-8258-5297-0

Karin Joggerst
Getrennte Welten – getrennte Geschichte(n)?
Zur politischen Bedeutung von Erinnerungskultur im israelisch-palästinensischen Konflikt. Im Anhang: Interviews mit Benny Morris, Ilan Pappe, Tom Segev, Moshe Zimmermann und Moshe Zuckermann
Im israelisch-palästinensischen Konflikt spielt die kollektive Erinnerung an die eigene Vergangenheit sowie der Umgang mit der Geschichte „des Anderen" eine zentrale Rolle für die Gegenwart und die Wahrnehmung des „Feindes". Der Rekurs auf die jeweilige Vergangenheit beider Kollektive basiert auf einer exklusiven Leidensgeschichte, die den anderen als Opfer negiert. Dabei bestimmt das Kollektivgedächtnis nicht nur das aktuelle Gegenwarts- und Geschichtsbewußtsein, sondern spiegelt in der Tradierung von Selbst- und Feindbildern auch zentrale Herrschaftsinteressen.
In diesem Buch geht die Verfasserin der Frage nach, welche politische Bedeutung der Erinnerungskultur im Konflikt und dessen möglicher Überwindung zukommt.

Bd. 6, 2002, 144 S., 15,90 €, br., ISBN 3-8258-5968-1

Heike Roggenthin
„Frauenwelt" in Damaskus
Institutionalisierte Frauenräume in der geschlechtergetrennten Gesellschaft Syriens
Die strikte räumliche Trennung weiblicher und männlicher Sphären und Räume sowie eine klare Rollenzuweisung charakterisieren die segregierte, segmentäre Gesellschaftsordnung des Vorderen Orients. Die Geschlechterordnung ließ neben der „Männeröffentlichkeit" eine „Frauenöffentlichkeit" entstehen, in welcher Frauenräume als integraler Teil der Gesellschaft entstanden. In der Arbeit werden häusliche informelle, außerhäusliche formelle Frauenräume sowie formelle Wohltätigkeitsorganisationen beschrieben und deren Bedeutung für die Damaszenerinnen dargelegt. Die Frauenöffentlichkeit bietet Hilfestellung und Rückhalt bei der Bewältigung des Alltags. Sie trägt zum Erhalt der hierarchisch gegliederten Gesellschaftsordnung bei.

Bd. 7, 2002, 288 S., 17,90 €, br., ISBN 3-8258-6188-0

Mustafa Gencer
Bildungspolitik, Modernisierung und kulturelle Interaktion
Deutsch-türkische Beziehungen (1908 – 1918)
Die bildungspolitische Zusammenarbeit zwi-

LIT Verlag Münster – Hamburg – Berlin – London
Grevener Str./Fresnostr. 2 48159 Münster
Tel.: 0251 – 23 50 91 – Fax: 0251 – 23 19 72
e-Mail: vertrieb@lit-verlag.de – http://www.lit-verlag.de

schen Deutschland und der sich von einem Vielvölkerstaat zum Nationalstaat entwickelnden Republik Türkei bildet den Gegenstand dieser Untersuchung. Jenseits der verstärkten politisch-militärischen Kooperation analysiert Mustafa Gencer die mentalitätsgeschichtlichen Aspekte der deutsch-türkischen Beziehungen. Das gesellschaftliche Modernisierungsprojekt sollte die Lebensphilosophie der Türken mit Begriffen wie *deutsche* Ordnung, Organisation, Pünktlichkeit und Arbeitsmoral vertraut machen. Deutsche Intellektuelle, Offiziere, Berater und Professoren leisteten einen wichtigen Beitrag zur Nationalisierung des politischen Denkens in der spätosmanischen Zeit.
Bd. 8, Frühj. 2003, ca. 320 S., ca. 30,90 €, br., ISBN 3-82582-6370-0

Ute Meinel
Die Intifada im Ölscheichtum Bahrain
Hintergründe des Aufbegehrens von 1994–98
Bd. 9, Frühj. 2003, ca. 360 S., ca. 35,90 €, br., ISBN 3-8258-6401-4

Whahit Wahdat-Hagh
Die Islamische Republik Iran
Die Herrschaft des politischen Islam als eine Spielart des Totalitarismus
Bd. 10, Frühj. 2003, ca. 608 S., ca. 35,90 €, br., ISBN 3-8258-6781-1

Politics and Economics in Africa
Series Editors: Robert Kappel and Ulf Engel
(Universität Leipzig)

Jedrzej Georg Frynas
Oil in Nigeria
Conflict and Litigation between Oil Companies and Village Communities
"Oil in Nigeria is destined to become a standard reference work on the Niger Delta and a template for future legal studies. Its relanvace extends beyond Nigeria and it deserves a wide readership." (African Affairs)
"An important study of the interplay among multinationals, local legal systems, and activists for human rights and the environment." (Foreign Affairs)
"I would highly recommend this book to everyone interested in understanding the complex story of the oil industry in Nigeria, the role of both the state and the oil companies and the impact of oil exploration on local communities in the Niger Delta." (Journal of Modern African Studies)
"The autor's approach is lateral and the narratives made clear with illustrations and conclusions, are compelling and revealing." (Social & Legal Studies)
"This carefully researched book … is of interest not only to specialists in Nigeria, but to anyone seeking to understand how international relations of diplomacy and business have adapted to the brave new world of privatisation." (Stephen Ellis, African Studies Centre Leiden)
Bd. 1, 2000, 288 S., 25,90 €, br., ISBN 3-8258-3921-4

Ulf Engel
Die Afrikapolitik der Bundesrepublik Deutschland 1949–1999
Rollen und Identitäten
Gibt es angesichts der Vielschichtigkeit der afrikapolitischen Beziehungen Bonns eine übergreifende Klammer für die Interpretation der westdeutschen Afrikapolitik? Auf der Basis einer als "empirischer Konstruktivismus" bezeichneten Wissenschaftsmethode werden in dieser Arbeit vier Interpretationsdimensionen bemüht: Rollen, Normen, der Prozeß der Normenaneignung und das Verhältnis von Identität und Paradigmenwechsel. Dabei steht die Frage im Vordergrund, wie sich afrikapolitische Identitäten konstituieren, reproduzieren oder verändern. Einem Überblickskapitel zu den dominanten politischen Paradigmen der Bonner Afrikapolitik folgen Fallstudien zur Anwendung der Hallstein-Doktrin gegenüber Tanzania (1964–65), zur Beteiligung der Bundesrepublik an der UN-Sicherheitsratsinitiative 435 zur Lösung der Namibiafrage (1973–83), zur im Rahmen der Europäischen Politischen Zusammenarbeit betriebenen Sanktionspolitik gegenüber Südafrika (1985/86) sowie zur Politik in Zentral- und Westafrika unter den Vorzeichen regionaler französischer Hegemonie, mit besonderer Berücksichtigung von Togo (1956–67 bzw. 1991–94).
Bd. 2, 2001, 344 S., 25,90 €, br., ISBN 3-8258-4709-8

Barbara Praetorius
Power for the People
Die unvollendete Reform der Stromwirtschaft in Südafrika nach der Apartheid
Bd. 3, 2001, 312 S., 25,90 €, br., ISBN 3-8258-4772-1

Ulf Engel; Robert Kappel (Eds.)
Germany's Africa Policy Revisited
Interests, images and incrementalism
Bd. 4, 2002, 224 S., 20,90 €, br., ISBN 3-8258-5985-1

LIT Verlag Münster–Hamburg–Berlin–London
Grevener Str./Fresnostr. 2 48159 Münster
Tel.: 0251–23 50 91 – Fax: 0251–23 19 72
e-Mail: vertrieb@lit-verlag.de – http://www.lit-verlag.de